Buying and
Renovating a House
in the City

Buying and Renovating a House in the City

A PRACTICAL GUIDE
Revised Edition

Deirdre Stanforth
and Martha Stamm Connell

HIPPOCRENE BOOKS
New York · 1985

For information, address: Hippocrene Books, Inc., 171 Madison Avenue, New York, NY 10016.

ISBN 0-87052-026-1

Printed in the United States of America.

Revised Edition, 1985
Originally Published, 1972

*This book is dedicated to
all those who have rescued
and restored old houses.*

Contents

Preface

THE ORIGINAL EDITION of this book, published in 1972, grew out of a need for information and encouragement for those interested in renovating deteriorating city houses as homes. It was the direct result of our experiences, augmented by a year of research and scores of interviews with others involved in renovation efforts across the country. At that time preservation was not widely accepted. Choosing to make a home and raise a family in the inner city was bad enough, but investing one's life's savings in the restoration of an old house in a shabby neighborhood was considered insane. In the past decade attitudes have changed dramatically. Local and national media have frequently illustrated the Cinderella transformation of neglected, abused buildings into stunning homes. Preservation has become popular nationwide, and owning an old house is not only acceptable, but even fashionable.

Because of the wider appreciation of the value and potential of period buildings in all types and vintages, *Buying and Renovating a House in the City* is needed now more than ever. Though the variety and scope of renovation has broadened, the basic problems involved remain un-

changed: understanding what to look for in the purchase of a house, planning a renovation, and dealing with real estate brokers, bankers, lawyers, architects, and contractors—or what you must be prepared to do if you prefer to do without them.
However, there have been changes that required revision of the original text. Due to soaring real estate prices and interest rates, new mortgage tables were necessary, and new types of financing, changing tax laws, and zoning regulations had to be explained.

Another change dictated the deletion of a hundred-page chapter called "A Tour of Renovation Neighborhoods," which was written primarily to inspire the lonely renovator. For at that time the venturesome urban pioneer had to surmount many obstacles: mortgage money and insurance were difficult or impossible to come by, and the government's conception of improving a neighborhood was limited to demolition. Neighborhoods undergoing spontaneous revival were largely unknown to each other, and there was little or no exchange of ideas or shared experience. We felt it was important and encouraging to know that others were not only trying but succeeding in a similar struggle. Fortunately, we no longer need to persuade people that renovating an old building is worthwhile, and so many neighborhoods have been revived since 1972 that this chapter is now as dated as last year's telephone book. Although these success stories continue to be exciting to us, a meaningful revision of this chapter would now require a full-length book.

A further consequence of the growing popularity of restoration is a new industry providing materials for old houses, and a new sensitivity of professionals who deal with them. When researching the original book, we asked a professor at the Yale School of Architecture how to find architects trained in renovation. His answer was,"There aren't any." And when the Stanforths called a recommended architect about restoring their brownstone, he replied somewhat scornfully, "I didn't go to school to be a plumber!" We are happy to report that this same man has become a noted restoration architect, and trustee of an organization that promotes preservation.

It has often been said that if you keep something long enough, it will come back in style. Though this referred to clothing, it applies equally well to architecture. Look at the houses in your city with a new awareness: today's "out of fashion" may be tomorrow's "in vogue."

We continue to believe strongly that the rewards of buying and renovating a house are worth all the effort. We hope that with the help of this book, the experience will be as painless as possible.

Happy Renovating!

DEIRDRE STANFORTH
MARTHA STAMM CONNELL

Buying and
Renovating a House
in the City

1 | Rediscovery of the City House

OWNING A HOME in Washington's Georgetown or Manhattan's Sutton Place or Turtle Bay is an unattainable dream for most of us, a privilege reserved for the very rich. But these prestigious addresses were once far from fashionable: they were down-at-the-heels, decaying neighborhoods, where a house could have been bought for next to nothing. And there are countless other reviving city communities that have undergone similar reversals in fortune.

Young families everywhere have discovered that they could create their own Georgetowns, many finding that they could buy more space than they could afford to rent, some even living rent-free in houses with twelve-foot ceilings, wood paneling, and marble mantels. Those with traditional tastes have enjoyed the opportunity of rescuing neglected period homes and restoring splendid architectural details to their original beauty. Others, who prefer a contemporary setting, have bought "shells" and gutted them to create dramatic new spatial environments.

Every city has houses as good as those in Georgetown or Turtle Bay, as structurally sound, as potentially beautiful,

The C. Jared Ingersoll's
eighteenth-century house
in Philadelphia's Society
Hill (facing page),
showing one room before
and another after resto-
ration. (facing page).

A house in Savannah's
Marshall Row before
and after restoration.

and often of greater historic value. The astonishing fact is that much of our architectural heritage had been left to die in our slums. How did it happen?

Cities originally grew around a center—town hall, churches, stores—with the homes of citizens erected nearby, clustered close together for convenience and safety. As cities prospered, the business sections spread outward, and the more affluent began to move. The first residential neighborhoods were abandoned for more fashionable ones. With the advent of the automobile, people were tempted to move even farther away to the new suburbs. In larger cities the creation of the apartment house lured others from private homes. Meanwhile, the early residential neighborhoods, deserted in this phased withdrawal and now considered totally undesirable, became housing for the desperately poor. Because of their poverty and the greed of absentee landlords, they were inevitably packed like the proverbial sardines into houses that had been built for one family. Result: slums.

Ironically, the automobile, which made possible the creation of the suburbs, has contributed to their undoing. By its very proliferation, the automobile began to strangle its own mobility, forcing commuters to spend hours on traffic-clogged expressways, traveling from suburban homes to city jobs. Urban sprawl has made suburbs almost indistinguishable from cities. The rural atmosphere that once lured city dwellers has been gradually vanishing in a pall of pollution.

The cycle was complete. People began to rediscover the center of the city as a place to live . . . in those lovely old houses that had been built as homes by their forefathers. Not only did these houses have charm and history; they were built to last, and despite the ravages of time and frightful abuse, were still more solid and substantial than anything built in the past several decades. Best of all, to the first who discovered them, they were cheap—because nobody wanted them. The larger ones were even adaptable

Capital Hill houses.

to provide home-plus-income.

Georgetown is a notable example of an entire community reborn in this manner. Today Georgetown is the top address in the nation's capital, the home of society and statesmen. However, in 1930, when the first young couple scraped together all their savings for the down payment on a run-down house in the midst of Georgetown's blight and deterioration, their family and friends thought they were crazy to want to live there, to invest their hard-earned money in such a shabby neighborhood. Two centuries ago, in 1751, Georgetown was born as a tiny village on the Potomac. Initially a tobacco port, it became one of the important shipping centers of the colonial period. By the time Washington was made America's capital in 1800, Georgetown, well established on its hill four miles away, was the thriving home of prosperous merchants and landowners. The streets of Washington were still mudholes when Pierre L'Enfant took up residence in a Georgetown tavern while creating his famous plan for the layout of the city. But the growth of Washington swallowed Georgetown, robbing it of its identity. Congress revoked its right to a separate government and finally even the use of its name.

The decline of Georgetown began with the Civil War, and by the 1920's all but a few families had moved away to newly fashionable neighborhoods. In the early thirties, when the first stirrings of the historic-preservation movement were beginning in Williamsburg, Charleston, and New Orleans, a few houses were bought and saved as museum pieces. The prices were low, and word spread to some of the bright young men who had been brought in to staff Franklin Roosevelt's New Deal. In those Depression days, the small-scaled bargain houses in Georgetown tempted young couples who could not afford new houses.

Financing was hard to come by. In the opinion of financiers, Georgetown property was being "overimproved" in relation to its value: their theory was that you should only upgrade to the level of the neighborhood. On this basis, Georgetown would have barely risen above slum level. But the new pioneers wanted quality equal to the best the suburbs had to offer. They made the most of the Georgian simplicity of architecture, enhancing it with bright new paint and carriage lamps, restoring the charming village atmosphere of tree-lined streets and brick sidewalks. Their instinct for quality was well rewarded, for their "overimprovement" played a large part in attracting newcomers and beginning a chain reaction. Their confidence was infectious, their enthusiasm created enthusiasm. Prices doubled and redoubled many times, proving that a rising neighborhood is the best investment of all.

The lesson of Georgetown showed that the transformation of a neighborhood can begin with one house, one block. Its influence was enormous in beckoning millions back to the cities.

The same story has been repeated nationwide—in Baltimore, Philadelphia, Pittsburgh, Richmond, Boston, Chicago, San Francisco, New York, and many other cities. The types of houses may vary, but the motivation and spirit are universal; and the problems are the same. As a front page story in the *National Observer* (December 15, 1969) put it, "For a growing number of young, educated, childbearing middle class Americans, happiness is a home in a slum. . . . The trend is national and unmistakable."

The trend began in the 1960's, a largely unnoticed countermovement to the flight to suburbia that had characterized the forties and fifties. National attention in the sixties was focused on urban renewal, as massive government programs and billions of dollars were poured into an effort to resurrect our dying cities. Emphasis was on demolition and rebuilding until at last there came a reaction against wanton destruction, as many Americans began to realize that most of our architectural heritage was being wiped out along with the slums. A country that made the worship of the new and the waste of the old a way of life suddenly became conservation- and preservation-minded. While millions traveled to Europe to admire old buildings, we began discovering some of our own were worth saving.

In 1960 the Washington *Star* wrote, "Pioneering restoration activity is almost always carried forward by private families of average means. . . . Optimism is a characteristic

Houses in Church Hill, Richmond, Virginia.

of the restorationist." Areas of many cities where no government programs existed were privately renewed by these optimistic families, who craved economic living space; and as a result, decaying neighborhoods underwent dramatic changes. The emerging new communities had a

Center city Philadelphia has many alleys like this one, lined with small houses imaginatively renovated.

sense of identity, pride, and purpose that no amount of government planning could have created.

Both the Stamms and the Stanforths and their counterparts in other cities sought out old houses in "bad" neighborhoods because that was where they could get the most for their money. It was simply a tremendous bonus that underneath cracked paint they found mahogany woodwork, under accumulated grime a marble vestibule, under layers of linoleum an intricate parquet floor. And the high ceilings with ornate plasterwork, the stained glass, elaborate wrought and cast iron, and beautiful bronze hardware! It was a great bonanza, like discovering buried treasure. It was really after the fact that they began to

Village atmosphere in downtown Philadelphia.

appreciate the quality and history of the houses they had bought. It was only out of sheer necessity that they became involved in improving their neighborhoods as well as their

Bolton Hill, Baltimore. Note brick sidewalks and typical marble steps.

Martha salvaged these wonderful bronze doorknobs which were under numerous layers of paint.

Early and late Victorian mantels. (above).

Late nineteenth-century parquet (facing page, below).

A

B

C

*Variety of doorways
found in old city houses:
A. Brooklyn Heights,
B. Savannah, C. West
Seventy-sixth Street,
Manhattan, D. Park
Slope, Brooklyn,
E. Newport, F. Stamm
house, Manhattan's Up-
per West Side, G. West
Eighty-fifth Street,
Manhattan.*

D

E

F

G

houses. It was just a happy accident that they had made investments in property that would multiply in value as their neighborhoods improved. And without realizing it, they were playing a role in the preservation of our architectural heritage. For even if individual houses were not

Pittsburgh facades.

of landmark quality, a block of restored houses can make a significant visual impact, and the reclamation of once-viable neighborhoods strengthens and revitalizes our cities while preserving our past.

Savannah clapboard row houses.

After it was repeatedly shown by enterprising families seeking affordable housing that the deterioration of old houses and their neighborhoods could be reversed, their value was recognized, and bargains became much more difficult to find. But most cities still have run-down areas where sound housing stock, often well-disguised by dirt, peeling paint, artificial siding, and tacked-on additions awaits discovery by the venturesome. Whether they are row houses or freestanding, architectural jewels or merely comfortable homes, elaborate mansions or workingman's cottages, the buildings from our past offer enterprising people the opportunity to create dwellings designed to fulfill their tastes and needs.

<table>
<tr><td>2</td><td>The Infinite Possibilities of Old Houses</td></tr>
</table>

THE OLDEST AMERICAN HOUSES still standing date back to the 1600's and early 1700's, but these are very rare indeed. More prevalent are the late eighteenth-century dwellings of New England, the stately clapboards of Providence and Newport, and the lovely brick colonials of Philadelphia and Alexandria. It is remarkable that so many have survived the ravages of time, deterioration, and the bulldozer. These houses were usually built freestanding, on narrow lots, with two stories, five rooms on each floor, laid out around a central chimney. Most were homes for well-to-do merchants and artisans and are ideally designed for family living. (They were, in fact, the prototype for many suburban homes.) Usually the objects of loving restoration, they need only the addition of modern conveniences in the form of plumbing, heating, wiring, bathrooms, and kitchens in order to be converted from charming eighteenth-century fossils to equally charming twentieth-century life.

However, it was the ubiquitous Victorian that attracted most of the renovation which sprang up spontaneously in the 1960's. Abundantly available and incredibly cheap because they had been disdained for half a century, these houses, built in all shapes and sizes (from cottage to mansion) in every American city, town, and hamlet, offered an opportunity to live in the grace and style of a bygone era on a relatively modest budget.

From the mid-nineteenth century to the early 1900's city streets were lined with Victorian row houses built of brick, stone, or wood. The building of entire blocks of houses in rows with party walls and identical façades was a style imported from England, where they are called "terrace

A double house in Newport, Rhode Island, lends itself to two-family contemporary living.

Transformation of Providence's Benefit Street, accomplished with removal of artificial siding and cobbled-on additions, and application of bright new paint.

San Francisco Victorian.

houses." Exteriors faced with brownstone (a roseate sand-stone) became so popular that row houses are often called "brownstones" no matter what material adorns the façades. Fashions and regional tastes eventually varied architectural styles and materials. Blocks were no longer designed as a unified whole: even one house might be a combination of several styles and materials. And although they continued to be built in rows, in many cities they were no longer joined together, but freestanding. In New Orleans their façades were adapted to the regional fashion with Greek revival columns and balconies decorated with ornate ironwork. And San Francisco created a row-house façade uniquely its own, adorned with elaborate redwood millwork in a variety of patterns, painted in bright colors, and affectionately christened the "Painted Ladies." But whether freestanding or connected with party walls, whether in Baltimore, Boston, New York, or Washington, the interior design was essentially the same. Constructed in a number of sizes, from two stories to five, and a variety of widths and depths, these houses are generally long and narrow, with major rooms, doors, and windows front and rear, and a stairway running up one side.

Non-row house Victorians did not conform to this layout, or any other standard floor plan, often defying symmetry and conformity with nooks, crannies, round rooms, and turret hideaways. But most Victorian interiors (except for the most modest cottages) were decorated with the same wonderful architectural details, usually ordered from catalogues, and therefore duplicated all over the country.

Mid-nineteenth century houses had simple wide plank pine flooring (usually covered with carpeting), marble mantels, and wide curved moldings for doors and window frames, with the Greek ear motif at the corners. A decade or so later, decoration increased, with plaster moldings and ceiling medallions, and parquet floors. In the 1890's, plaster and marble were replaced by dark woodwork, which was paneled, inlaid, carved, turned, and the more ornate, the better. Late Victorian houses were embellished with spooled woodwork and curlicues, louvered shutters that folded back into recesses on either side of the windows, etched or stained glass, marble washbasins or marble flooring in foyers, elegant pier mirrors, and filigree-patterned brass or bronze hardware. And most of those built between the 1870's and 1890's have exquisite parquet floors with elaborate borders. Often they can be discovered under countless layers of linoleum in homes converted to rooming houses, and with a minimum of refinishing they can be restored to their original beauty.

Wide moldings used in typical inner front door of Brooklyn house. Doors are two inches thick with beveled glass panels.

Mid-nineteenth-century wide plank flooring (below).

Behind almost austere exteriors is found extravagantly handsome plaster work, floor-length windows, wide moldings, and marble mantels—here lovingly restored by writer L. J. Davis in Brooklyn's Boerum Hill. Similar architectural details are found nationwide.

High Victorian decoration in Brooklyn (above) and Georgia (facing page).

As the Victorian has returned to favor, with prices rising accordingly, the bargain-conscious renovator has turned to post-Victorian houses, particularly the bungalow. The bungalow style, which came into being as a part of the Arts and Crafts movement of the late nineteenth century, was a reaction to the flamboyance of the Victorian house and reflected a changing way of life. Unlike high Victorian design, which presupposed cheap labor and an abundance of domestic help, the bungalow was designed for a simpler, more family-oriented life-style with a floor plan based on convenience for the housekeeper.

A variety of bungalow styles.

Because the bungalow was a prevalent force in single-family residential construction for the first two decades of the twentieth century, it can be found in abundance in most cities. And whether it is a modest workingman's house or a large mansion-type home, the bungalow's compact one to one-and-a-half-story floor plan works well today. The American bungalow, featuring low pitched roof with wide overhangs and comfortable front porch, is built of natural materials (stone, brick, wood, and shingle). Set back from the street with an ornamental front yard, it has a larger rear yard intended as a service area and playground for children, and perhaps a garden as well.

The floor plan always consists of living room with fireplace, formal dining room, a kitchen designed to be used by the housewife, two or more bedrooms, and one bath. Ceiling heights are nine or ten feet, and rooms are planned with cross ventilation in mind. Architectural details are simple. Interiors have hardwood floors with inlaid borders, built-in seats and bookshelves on either side of the fireplace, built-in china cabinets and breakfast nooks between dining room and kitchen, exposed ceiling beams, and simple articulation of door and window frames. Living rooms and dining rooms often feature varnished wainscoting, varying from window-sill level to three-quarters room-height, topped by dish shelves for displaying family treasures. Some living rooms even boast cathedral ceilings.

Exterior features include decorative chimney caps, exposed rafters under wide eaves, fancy patterns in masonry underpinnings, masonry bases for wooden porch columns, elaborate geometry in small-paned upper windows, and decorative brackets under the gable overhang.

The appeal of this house style is that the floor plan works well for today's living. The small two-bedroom houses make ideal first homes, and larger bungalows are suitable for growing families. Modernizing a kitchen, updating wiring, and decorating are often all that is needed.

Victorian exterior.

These Victorian cottages are located in the Columbus Historic District, Georgia, but similar examples can be found in many American cities.

Old houses can be full of surprises, not only because of architectural treasures that may be found under layers of paint or linoleum, but in terms of imaginative treatment by renovators. Although the exterior may remain unchanged, you never know what to expect inside. It is quite possible to find, side by side, two identical facades with unbelievably different worlds (even different centuries) behind the front doors. But it is not only conventional houses that have been transformed by innovation and ingenuity. Attractive homes have emerged from gas stations, firehouses,

Behind this typical nineteenth-century brownstone facade is a spectacular contemporary apartment designed by Caswell Cooke (facing page). When this house was purchased from the New Haven Redevelopment Agency, it had an interior in bad condition and there was nothing worth saving.

Neglected, ruined eighteenth-century Providence clapboard rescued and restored to its simple beauty and original function as a home.

bakeries, factories and warehouses, school houses and churches, as well as the more traditional barns and carriage houses.

There are three approaches to renovation:

1. Authentic restoration
2. Gutting and redesigning the interior
3. Partial restoration

Restoration can be the most rewarding: an old house is like a fine antique whose best features mellow with age. And as in the refinishing of antiques, removing every scratch and nick from an old house may diminish its character. In fact, old houses with every flaw erased and plaster walls and ceilings replaced, are often indistinguishable from new houses. Sometimes their attributes are not readily apparent, and therefore it is better, if possible, to live in a house and become familiar with it before making

any changes. "We went slowly, and let the house speak to us" is a sentiment expressed in a number of different ways by wise renovators.

A couple bought five acres in Louisiana, planning to demolish the derelict house that stood on the grounds. But before it was too late, they learned that the building was not only structurally sound but a rare example of early regional architecture with exceptional detailing. So they restored the house to its original splendor, and they are the proud possessors of a historic treasure.

On the other hand, a woman who bought one of the classic eighteenth-century clapboards on Benefit Street in Providence, Rhode Island, acted in haste and lived to regret it. Removing walls in a plan to redesign the layout, she discovered that nothing seemed to work. Finally, she said, "The house began screaming 'put me back.'" And that is what she did, but she wasted a great deal of money, and lost the two hundred-year-old plaster walls. Another irreversible loss she bitterly regrets was the beehive oven in the fireplace, which the contractor persuaded her must be removed in order to make the fireplace work properly. In hindsight, she "wished the Providence Preservation Society had tied me to a chair until they had explained how the house should be treated."

Architects and contractors are not always sensitive to restoration and may take the easy way out if the owner does not have a strong mind, firm control, and constantly supervises what is being done. The easy way is not always the best way in renovating an old house. How do you know how your vintage house should look? If your house is in an area that has a preservation organization, by all means avail yourself of their advice. Research libraries can be helpful, and *The Old House Journal* is an excellent source of information. Visit houses of the same period in your area. If they have been well handled, you will have an example to emulate; and if not, sometimes another's mistakes can effectively show you what *not* to do. Enough exposure will open your eyes to what is right or wrong in period homes. It is particularly important to be sensitive to appropriate exterior treatment: an outlandish paint color can ruin the appearance of an entire block. If your house is in a historic district, any exterior changes, including paint color and inappropriate windows and doors, may be disapproved by a review board.

For those whose taste runs to the traditional, there are still houses to be found with all the original details intact that can be restored to make lovely homes. However, there are some that either have no architectural detail left to save or had none to begin with. These provide the perfect opportunity for imaginative architectural design; a totally new spatial arrangement can be created within the shell of exterior walls.

Combining old and new is probably the most common method of exploiting the potential of old houses. Often a few pieces of carved woodwork or molded plaster can be more effectively set off by a starkly simple background or a natural brick wall than they were in their original setting. Some renovators prefer to play up whatever details exist and surround them with a contemporary setting rather than going the route of authentic restoration or gutting to the bone.

There is another alternative for filling in the gaps where pieces are missing, or even for providing decoration where none exists. What does a renovator do when he needs a

Dramatic contemporary interior created by Gerard Cugini in an old house in Boston's North End.

paneled door or some brass hardware? He goes in search of someone else's discards. In the 1960's, when the interest in renovation was just beginning, many of us were scavengers. It was quite common to find handsome mahogany front doors, newel posts, shutters, even mantels and cast iron firebacks thrown out on the sidewalk with the rubbish. Some early renovators acquired marvelous collections of jewel-like bronze doorknobs and hinges in a dazzling array of patterns, discarded by disinterested developers or housewreckers. Those days are just about gone. Even if they fail to appreciate the beauty of these decorative artifacts, most renovators now recognize the resale value. While it is still possible to find a mantel being sold by one renovator to another, usually via classified ads in the newsletters of preservation organizations, the primary source of replacement parts today is the salvage yard. If you happen to see a period house being demolished, you might ask the contractor to give or sell you pieces that you need. But chances are you will be competing with one of the businesses that now buy from wrecking companies for resale. By all means go and shop in any salvage outlets in your area. They are often filled with everything from doorknobs to chandeliers to wall paneling from entire rooms. You might even design a renovation around some of the beautiful parts available; but look before your plans are completed so that door frames can be built to fit the doors you buy, or window openings to fit the shutters—it seldom works the other way around.

If you cannot find original replacement parts, you may seek out reproductions. A whole new industry has evolved to meet the demand. Reproductions are now made by a number of companies selling ceiling medallions, ornamental moldings, pilasters, mantels, hardware, lighting fixtures, wallpaper, and so forth. A definitive catalogue of sources of these products, *A Buyer's Guide for the Pre-1939 House,* is published by The Old House Journal, 69A Seventh Avenue, Brooklyn, New York, 11217.

The Story of Two Renovations

SINCE MOST PEOPLE are amateurs when they tackle a renovation, it isn't until after they have finished that they realize the mistakes they have made and how they could have done better. There is a tremendous need for pooling the knowledge of those who have learned the hard way about the problems that lie in the path of a renovator, so that he need not stumble through them depending on luck—which can be bad as often as good. Few people really understand the very important financing of a house and the many different choices available. You might blunder into the right choice, but why take a chance? You could be stuck with the consequences of misinformed judgment for years to come. Did you know that a more expensive house could be a better buy than a comparable cheaper one, or did you think that purchase price was the only factor to consider?

You will probably need the help of at least some professionals, and you should know the scope of the services they provide in order to decide whether you need them or can do without them. Do you know what to expect of real estate brokers, architects, and contractors, and how to choose them and use them? Would you really be saving money by eliminating an architect and doing your own contracting? And if you choose to do it that way, do you know the right order in which the work should be done and the consequences of doing the wrong things first? Our objective is to inform you thoroughly about all of these and other elements that make for the successful renovation of a house.

We propose to pass along the knowledge we have accumulated, exposing potential traps, pitfalls, and mistakes in the buying and renovation of an old house, so that you can avoid the problems, making your own decisions on an enlightened basis. There is no better illustration than our own experiences to show you what can happen to well-educated, intelligent people who plunge in with inadequate preparation. Although our stories took place some years ago, they are as pertinent as ever; renovators today and tomorrow face the same problems. But it is not necessary to suffer to achieve a wonderful home. Be thoroughly prepared with all the knowledge you can glean; take advantage of our experience and research, talk to renovators, take your time.

• THE STAMM'S STORY

When Martha and Charlie Stamm decided to buy a house in Manhattan, they had small savings and a modest income. They had moved back to a city apartment after two years of suburban home ownership, but two years later, with a third child on the way, they needed more space. An unsuccessful search for a larger apartment they could afford led them to consider buying a brownstone on the blighted Upper West Side. Prices there were low, and if they had rental income from half of a four- or five-story house, the monthly cost after renovation would be about the same or less than that of a small suburban development house, and the cash investment in the finished house would be low.

However, the condition of West Side houses ranged from clean but antiquated to overcrowded and unfit for human habitation to boarded-up and stripped of everything save the beams. For seven months Martha looked at every available house in a twenty-block area, climbing hundreds of flights of stairs, sometimes guided only by a flashlight. She asked innumerable questions, gathered information, worked out various floor plans adaptable to most houses, and became very realistic about what they could afford. Finally, only a few weeks before the baby was born, there was an ad in the paper for the right house at the right price.

It was a Sunday afternoon in August when the Stamms went to see the house on West 78th Street. Hot summer weekends bring out the worst in blighted neighborhoods, but Martha did not notice the trash-littered street, the overcrowded and unsightly houses, or the noisy swarms of people sitting on stoops and hanging out of open windows. She saw only the unbroken line of row houses in an amazing variety of architectural styles, terminating in a park at the rear of the American Museum of Natural History. Her vision of the potential beauty of the block blotted out the sordid reality.

The house was painted a vile pinkish-beige, dirtied by soot over the years. The handsome two-inch-thick double-entry doors at the top of the stoop were disguised under innumerable coats of peeling paint. The interior however, was clean and freshly painted. The owner lived in part of the house and rented out the rest to roomers. The door of his apartment, standing a full ten feet high, had been stripped to its natural mahogany splendor and was set off with an expensive new doorknob.

The house was no castle. It still had the original 1889 plumbing and fixtures, with every shape and size of footed bathtub and an old wooden-tank, pull-chain toilet. How-

Fanciful details of Upper West Side brownstone facades.

46

ever, compared to the other houses they had seen, it looked like a mansion. The price was right. The cash was low. They could move in immediately and renovate whenever they were ready. There was even a public school across the street for the children.

Early Monday they called a corporate attorney friend, seeking his recommendation for a real estate lawyer. His reaction was "You must be crazy. That's the worst thing you could possibly do!" There followed a lecture on why they should not buy real estate in Manhattan, much less on the West Side. After failing to dissuade them, he reluctantly sent them to see a real estate attorney. And so the Stamms found an invaluable lawyer, bought a house, hired an architect, had a baby and moved into their new-old house— all within two months.

It was not until moving day when they found a house already full of furniture that they realized the house had been sold furnished. Everything except their beds had to be stacked in one room, and by the end of the day it looked like a storage warehouse. The five Stamms owned four double beds, six single beds, one set of bunk beds, and a crib, plus innumerable tables and chairs.

They had no idea of the frustrations that lay ahead of them, and they did not care. To them the house was beautiful, even with its half-dozen sinks and stoves, decrepit furniture, and old plumbing that sprang a leak every day or two. They explored every inch, discovering lovely doorknobs hidden under layers of paint and stamped brass hinges on every door.

Looking back now with the knowledge she has since acquired, Martha realizes they were very foolish in many ways, and frightfully ignorant. They purchased a house without adequate cash to pay for the renovation. A personal loan from an out-of-state bank gave them enough money to buy and begin the conversion. This loan was short-term and interest-bearing only, and had to be renewed three times in two years before they were able to

The Stamm's ground-floor living room was originally the kitchen in their 1889 Manhattan brownstone. To maximize the eight-foot ceiling height, they removed the ceiling to expose the structural beams. Textured plaster was applied to the walls, and a new fireplace was created from the existing flue. Glass Dutch doors replaced windows to provide more light and give access to the enclosed garden.

pay it off. It could have been canceled at any time, leaving them up the proverbial creek.

The Stamms knew absolutely nothing about construction financing, which would have enabled them to renovate with far less financial strain. They were aware that the property could be refinanced when the renovation was complete, so they could repay the out-of-state loan, but they did not know how they would get from point A (purchase) to point B (completion and refinancing) with the little money they had.

The lack of money, though it caused them untold anxiety, was in some ways a blessing. It meant that they had to weigh every penny to be sure they got their money's worth. It also meant living in the house while the work was being done, which made them aware of every nail that was driven and every stud erected. The knowledge of construction Martha absorbed while observing and asking questions, and the close relationship she developed with the workmen, enabled her with no prior experience to see that all work was done properly. The importance of supervision became obvious, and Martha was thankful she was forced to be present constantly. Whenever a question arose (the plans and specifications gave only the barest essentials), the workmen could ask Martha.

The Stamms' financial situation also prevented them from letting their contractor get ahead of them. They could scarcely make regular payments, let alone make them before the work was done. They took out a personal loan, borrowed on insurance policies, got the existing second mortgage slightly increased, and cut their expenses to the bare bones in order to save money for construction payments. When things began to look really desperate, they unexpectedly inherited a small sum of money sufficient to pay for the remaining construction.

The plans for renovation were complete and approved by the city about a month after the Stamms moved in. The construction budget had to be very low, but the first bids were more than double the amount they had planned. Despair over the high bids finally made them see the block as it was. They now understood why friends who came to visit were so strangely quiet when taken on a tour of the house as the Stamms proudly explained which walls would be removed, where the new kitchen would go, and how the mudhole in back would be transformed into an oasis of greenery. Depression was a mild word for their mood. It was about this time that the doorbell rang and Martha was greeted by a menacing-looking stranger. Thoroughly scared, she wished she had followed advice about not opening the door unless she knew who was there. Then she realized what he was saying: he lived across the street and had seen her children sitting on the window ledge upstairs. He was afraid they would fall, and thought she ought to know. After thanking him profusely and soundly spanking the children, she decided that all was not wrong with the world. She realized she felt safer in her run-down seedy block than anywhere else she had lived in Manhattan. She might not approve of the overcrowded rooming houses, but the tenants would not harm her or her family. It was a good block and there were good people living on it. They would renovate their house and do it well. And their block would look like the block she had visualized that Sunday afternoon in August. It would not be easy, but they could do it.

They did find a contractor they could afford, and they accepted his bid without even thinking of checking his credentials. As it turned out, the Stamms were incredibly lucky. The contractor was a young man just starting in business for himself. He and the Stamms had a lot of learning to do together, but they were eager and willing.

There were many problems: a carpenter who did not know how to use a miter box, and consequently moldings that did not meet at the corners; tile men who walked off the job because they had not been paid; a plumber who let a gallon of filthy water drop in the middle of their bed when he removed a sprinkler pipe; hot and cold water lines were reversed, so that Charlie froze when he took his first shower. But the contractor was willing to rectify mistakes as soon as they were discovered.

The five Stamms lived in two rooms, cooking on a two-burner hot plate, washing dishes in the bathtub. As the family moved about to allow work to be done, there were times when the only closet was on the top floor while the beds were on the ground floor. The telephone remained installed on the parlor floor, although they did not occupy that floor for nearly seven months.

They had originally planned to finish their own apartment on the lower two floors, leaving the remainder until a later date. After construction began, the contractor pointed out that it would be much cheaper to finish the entire house at once. So they revised their schedule to finish the rental unit first: the income would help pay for completion of their own apartment.

Renovation began December eighth, and by July they were ready to rent the apartment on the third and fourth floors. The second Sunday they advertised, it was rented easily. With rent coming in steadily, the Stamms could get on with the job of finishing their own apartment.

During the course of renovation, Martha became one of the prime movers in the revival of the neighborhood. She helped found a block association, and a campaign was started to plant trees along the sidewalk. Long-time property owners at first resisted, certain that the children and bums would destroy the trees, but when those planted by newcomers in the spring were still thriving in the fall, everyone joined in, and thirty-five trees were planted.

The block association also worked with police and sanitation departments to rid the block of pushers, prostitutes, and garbage. People began taking an interest in their surroundings. When the Stamms and several newcomers painted the exteriors of their houses, other owners must have made the same observation as the Stamm's five-year-old: "But it makes the other houses look so dirty!" Seven other houses were painted the following month, and the whole atmosphere on the block began to change.

Within four years the Stamms had bought and renovated five houses on their block. Three were purchased to upgrade and rent or resell to resident owners. Then they sold their first house in order to buy and renovate a larger building that looked more like a candidate for demolition than renovation. By a combination of gutting, salvaging, and scavenging, they made the most of the interior space, using all the knowledge gained from the previous renovations to create an apartment that provided for the increased needs of the family. They were experienced enough to work out proper financing, contract for the job to be completed before moving in, and plan the rental units in such a way that they could live rent-free in half the house. The amount of cash invested in the property was only about 20 percent of the finished cost, and the finished cost was about 30 percent below the market value of the completed house.

· THE STANFORTH'S STORY

Deirdre and Jim Stanforth were facing eviction from their second home in eight years. Both were large, rambling, high-ceilinged apartments in old rent-controlled buildings on Manhattan's Upper East Side, and both fell victim to the wrecker's ball. The Stanforths could not face searching for another such apartment in view of the fate of the previous two. Jim did not rule out the suburbs, but Deirdre would not consider it. She had come to New York because she loved it, and she was determined to live right in the midst of it, where she could take advantage of museums and theaters whenever she had the inclination.

The Stanforths had flirted with the idea of buying a town house twelve years earlier, but then they found their first large, cheap, rent-controlled apartment, and the moment passed. By this time, East Side houses had tripled in price and were out of the question, even though the Stanforths had squirreled away considerable cash. Then they heard tempting stories about the brave new pioneers who were buying houses for fantastically low prices on the West Side. This area had a frightening image to many New Yorkers because of countless news reports of poverty, filth, and crime, and the gang wars of *West Side Story*.

They started out by "casing" the area, driving skeptically back and forth from 70th through 96th Streets, taking notes on each block, rating its degree of acceptibility. It was obvious that some blocks were struggling to make a comeback, with a few buildings visibly cleaned up, but others were a disaster. They decided to look at some houses, though it was appalling to consider pouring their life's savings into such a disreputable neighborhood.

The turning point came when they visited a renovated house and met the owners, who were anxious to encourage

The Stanforth's living room after renovation.

more homeowners to join them. When the Stanforths saw the splendid interior of the restored home, they were convinced. Soon after, they found a house; a narrow four-story house, one of a row of four built in 1881 with matching brownstone façades and columned porticoes. The small front parlor had a lovely herringbone-patterned parquet floor with an inlaid ribbon border, and a foot-wide

Unusual location of stairway provides exceptionally large foyer, making the narrow fifteen-foot house seem much wider than it is. Needless to say, this picture was taken after renovation.

plaster frieze with wreaths and crossed torches above the picture molding. The living room had wood-paneled walls and a high-beamed ceiling.

Although they liked the house when they first saw it, they felt no sense of urgency until a few days later, when the broker said it was sold. Then (oh, the perversity of human nature) they knew they wanted it. It seemed exactly the right house, and the opportunity was lost. But within a week the broker called to say that the new owner, a speculator, was willing to sell.

After another visit it was agreed that the house was indeed worth negotiating for, and with the broker's help, they were able to reach agreement on a good price, in spite of the considerable profit being made by the speculator. But before they signed a contract and became irrevocably involved, they went through the final throes of soul searching. Jim spent several evenings sitting in their car until after midnight, watching to see what happened in the block. A doorman around the corner on Central Park West said they were out of their minds even to consider it; the street was a hotbed of addicts and prostitutes. The owners of two of the respectable-looking houses in the block were more encouraging. In short, the Stanforths went through a great deal of agonizing, but were convinced that the West Side was on its way back.

Their contract specified that the building be delivered vacant (they had never been able to see the top floors, which were full of roomers), and a date was set for closing four months later. The broker offered his help in obtaining mortgages, but they felt that real estate brokers were about as trustworthy as used-car dealers, so they turned his offer down. They realized afterward that this was stupid: brokers often expect to give this service, and there is nothing to lose by considering whatever financing assistance they can offer.

The mortgage was obtained from a savings and loan association: based on plans for the house, it would pay one-third at closing, one-third halfway through construction, and the final third on completion. Meanwhile, work had begun with an architect, who had assured them that the renovation could be done within their budget. They had only considered a single-family house, but as there was a superfluous room on the ground floor front, it occurred to them that they could create a small efficiency apartment there.

The architect's preliminary sketches presented three plans: one providing for a single-family house; another containing an efficiency rental apartment; and a third including a three-and-a-half-room split-level rental apartment using only the one room on the ground floor plus half the cellar. This last scheme involved excavating the rear garden to the cellar-floor level (which was three-quarters underground) and opening the back wall with French doors onto the garden. The plan created a thirty-foot living room and small kitchen in the cellar level, with bedroom, bath, and private entrance under the stoop upstairs. The Stanforths would have access to the garden by a stairway from their kitchen. This use of a cellar was most unusual at the time, but has since become extremely popular, because it utilizes valuable wasted space.

A contract was signed with the architect to start work immediately so that construction could begin as soon as the house was theirs. But it was not until four months after the closing that demolition actually began. Two months after closing, plans and specifications finally went out to contractors for bids—and bidding took another two months. Actually, more time should have been taken, but knowing they faced impending eviction from their apartment, they felt they could not afford to waste another day. (It is vital to *take* time at this stage, because a mistake in choosing a contractor can be fatal.)

The bids came in as high as four times the amount they had set as their limit. Shocked, they sat down with the architect to cut out everything not absolutely necessary be-

Identical before and after views of garden apartment—fireplace replaces furnace.

Garden before and after. Flagstones were found on and under the ground and laid by Stanforths. Most plants were donated from friend's country property—forest ferns thrive in city shade.

fore negotiating with the two lowest bidders, whose price was merely twice what they were prepared to spend. They chose one of the two and tried to check on him. He was far from solid financially, but at least seemed to be honest. They were on the verge of signing with him when the second contractor dropped his bid by several thousand dollars to get the job. Naively, they felt they had achieved a tremendous bargain.

Their worst mistake was the innocent assumption that it is always possible to make a contractor live up to the terms of the contract. By then they felt so pressed for time that they did not check the second contractor beyond calling a few of his alleged suppliers and asking the bank to investigate his corporation. They did not wait for the result, but when they got it, it simply said that no record could be found of such a corporation. A corporation with no record and no actual place of business is one to avoid. The Stanforths' contractor was operating out of the addresses where his jobs were located, with no directory listing, only an answering service for a phone number. This was indicative of nothing but trouble.

Their next mistake was Jim's admonition to leave the workmen alone. Deirdre forced herself to stay away, when in fact she should have been on hand to supervise at every possible moment. If she had been on the premises, she would have realized the contractor was a crook. The fact that the work came out as well as it did must have been due to the architect's supervision. However, something went seriously awry in his control of the payment schedule. They had to depend on him because they had no idea when 25 percent of the carpentry was done or whether the plumbing and wiring were being installed correctly. The only safe way to use a contractor is always to keep the work ahead of the payments.

The demolition went very fast, but it always does. Their contractor did not stop altogether after that, but worked long enough to set them up for the *coup de grace*. He knew they would soon be homeless, and he knew how to use that to his advantage. The job he started in June was supposed to be finished in October. Some time after that deadline, fewer and fewer men were found working on the house, until at last, one weekday afternoon, no one was working at all. Panic set in, with the hot breath of the eviction marshal on their necks.

They consulted the architect, who advised against firing their contractor and getting another one, saying it would cost more in time and money. He sent the contractor a registered letter threatening to fire him if he did not perform. This tactic *seemed* to work: he reappeared at once, explaining that he was completely broke because the extender plumbers' strike (which had paralyzed union construction in the city for months) had prevented his finishing three jobs and collecting large sums of money he was owed. Therefore he could not meet his payroll or buy materials for their house. If the Stanforths would agree to meet those costs as they arose, he could get on with the work. The architect thought the request sounded reasonable, and in desperation they agreed.

They made out checks directly to suppliers and met the weekly payroll, subsequently found to be heavily padded. The full amount of the contract price was exhausted, and with the aid of a lawyer they extracted notes from the contractor for several thousand dollars more, to be advanced as a loan to continue the work. There was still too much work to be done for that amount to complete it; but he insisted that he had money coming in with which he would finish. He even signed an extraordinary document in which he agreed to complete a staggering list of items before they moved in the following week or pay a penalty of two hundred dollars a day. They have never been able to collect on either piece of paper.

Fortunately, working all weekend, his men managed to install the furnace, so there was heat and hot water. There was also one nearly complete bathroom and two painted bedrooms on the top floor. Otherwise the house was a shambles. Jim insisted the house was not fit to live in and that they must go to a hotel or stay with friends, but Deirdre preferred to stay on the scene watching what was happening than to go somewhere else and worry about it. So one week before Christmas they moved into the top floor of the unfinished house, and the contractor departed the same day, leaving behind a full crew of unpaid workmen. The Stanforths had no choice but to pay them and keep them on to finish the house, and that is what they did.

The Stanforths met with the architect in their new "home" to plan the salvage action. He was distressed about his part in the debacle and agreed to forego part of his fee and come around daily to instruct the workmen. He fulfilled his promise, and between them they managed to finish the house. The workmen arrived before eight every day including Saturdays, and the plasterer even worked Christmas and New Year's Day. If Deirdre was not up before they arrived, they would knock on the bedroom door to ask for instructions. Jim retired at night with his father-in-law's sword cane under the bed, ready to rise to his family's defense at any strange sound, because the rear of the house was virtually wide open. Deirdre was seen in nothing but paint-smeared blue jeans and sweater for months, and she often used their car as a truck to pick up extra bags of plaster and other assorted materials. She was so busy she did not have time to worry about the disreputable-looking people on the block.

They felt like refugees that Christmas. When Deirdre's mother arrived for her annual Christmas visit, she described their town house as a "disaster area." It was bad enough camping out with no kitchen for two months, but worse by far was finding the money to meet the payroll every week. Without financial help from the family, they would have been lost. They could easily have forfeited everything if they had had to sell the house in that condition, and they had nowhere else to live.

Meanwhile, with ever-mounting fury, they were discovering what a thief the contractor was and how little they could do about it. They were appalled to learn that the district attorney and attorney general's offices would do nothing at all, and that the contractor who cheated them was continuing to do the same, or worse, to others. All kinds of people began calling at their house to find him (including policemen to whom he had given a rubber check for protection). They got calls from two different banks that had given him loans on the same car! But worst of all, were the suppliers and subcontractors he had not paid who were threatening to put liens on the house. Not only had they already paid him what was owed these people, but it was possible that some materials had not even gone into their house. When credit is exhausted at one job, dishonest contractors often have material delivered and charged at another—then simply move it to where they need it. (This practice is called "kiting.")

They cleared up the liens themselves, by proving they had paid the full contract price before the claims were presented and therefore were not liable. However, this is a situation that should never arise: receipted bills, or a waiver of liens for all labor and supplies, should be presented by the contractor before he is paid.

The Stanforths completed the work on their house within three months after they moved in, and they rented their newly created apartment with no difficulty a month later. In spite of the misery it had caused them, they began to enjoy their house before they got rid of the last workman. Envious friends began dropping in, one of whom bought the rooming house next door even after hearing about their disasters. There was no problem attracting prospective homeowners to the neighborhood, because people kept coming to them. Remembering what a difference it made to see the interior of a renovated house, they welcomed every interested stranger. Although there were already four private houses on the block, there had been little visible change until their renovation. Probably the timing was right, but after that the trickle became a tidal wave. The prices of similar houses nearly tripled in three years, as approximately fifteen renovations got under way on their block alone.

Though they certainly never meant to, they became very involved in their community as leaders of the block association. Soon there were twenty-two new trees and high-intensity streetlights installed in the block. The pleasure of living in their house has continued to increase to the point where they feel it is the best decision they ever made. They have watched with astonishment as the surrounding area has undergone an incredible transformation. There was nowhere to eat at all that dreadful Christmas when they moved into the house without a functioning kitchen: now once-dreary Columbus Avenue has become an immensely popular restaurant row. Neighborhood brownstones and co-ops are in great demand, selling at astronomical prices. This means that their house is worth at least five times what they invested in it, and the rental of their small apartment more than covers monthly expenses. They consider themselves very lucky indeed.

4 | Living in Renovation Neighborhoods

WHAT KINDS OF PROBLEMS have renovators faced as pioneers in deteriorated city neighborhoods? Surprisingly few, on the whole. We usually learn that although our neighbors may be different from us, they are generally nice people. Everyone, including the poor, would like to get rid of the undesirable element—the pushers, prostitutes, and muggers. However, we come to learn that there is an advantage to living in a diversified neighborhood rather than an entirely homogeneous one, where there is a real loss of what Jane Jacobs, in her classic book *The Death and Life of Great American Cities,* calls "eyes on the street." There were many instances of such vigilance in the block that Martha Stamm moved into: a window-watching couple warning a widow that they saw a man get into her cellar; a caretaker calling the police in time to catch a prowler who broke into a vacant building. People who go out to work every day are busy with their own affairs and simply do not watch the street or take an interest in other people's problems. And when too many buildings are converted to small apartments, the more or less transient population does not care about or have a stake in the community.

There is a crime problem today in all American cities, and in some suburbs as well. The emerging Adams-Morgan renovation neighborhood in Washington, D.C., was particularly hard-hit by a crime wave resulting from an upheaval in another area. Refusing to be driven out of their newly renovated homes, the people banded together to fight back. Led by enterprising homeowner, Tedson Myers, they cut back sidewalk hedges that had acted as a screen for muggers, and installed floodlights so that their streets were daylight-bright at night. This solution was so effective that no further serious incidents occured. In Brooklyn's Park Slope, a series of purse snatchings was halted by a community plan in which everyone wore police whistles to be blown by victims or observers so that help could be summoned quickly. It worked, and the crimes stopped.

Where there is a persistent, ongoing crime problem, some New York City block associations have hired their own uniformed guards on a permanent basis, posting a sign warning criminals that the block is patrolled. It is certainly an effective solution, but one that requires a strong block association to follow through on the continuing task of collecting financial contributions from residents to pay the guard's salary.

A well-organized block association with good leadership is unquestionably the most effective tool for improving a neighborhood. The motto of our country—"In unity there is strength"—is proved over and over again in countless renovation communities. There is no better way to accomplish neighborhood improvement than by the organized efforts of like-minded people. It seems to happen almost spontaneously in most renovation areas. A few homeowners and caring tenants get together and a block association is born. As a result, block parties are given to promote community spirit and neighborliness or raise money for trees and window boxes, and house tours are planned to excite the interest of others in buying homes in the area.

Changing the image of the neighborhood is the root of the problem. Bad reputation and loss of pride lead to a lack of interest on the part of police, sanitation department, and city officials and to a defeatist attitude among residents. People who have lived in these neighborhoods for a long time have often given up trying; and yet, encouraged by newcomers' successes, they usually participate. A case in point was Martha Stamm's summoning police to end an outdoor crap game in her block. The first reaction was surprise, shock, and disapproval; however, the result was that other residents began to follow suit by taking action themselves.

The problem of public schools is unquestionably worse in some cities than in others. However, not all city schools are as bad as they are painted, and they will only be improved by parents who care; who become involved and demand better education. On the other hand, renovators often find that they can save money from what they would normally pay for housing, commuting, or a second car to send their children to private schools if they so desire.

Despair-breeding discouragement accelerated the downfall of neighborhoods; and reversal of the trend is bringing them back to life. There is not the slightest doubt that improvement begets improvement, confidence instills confidence, and enthusiasm inspires enthusiasm. The importance of visible improvement cannot be overstressed. A sidewalk littered with debris and garbage, or walls marked with graffiti invariably invite more of the same. Even one freshly painted house with a few handsome accessories and plantings can encourage imitation by other residents and inspire the purchase and upgrading of nearby properties by new owners. The first venturesome pioneers who renovate in a rundown neighborhood can achieve miracles, often instigating the renaissance of large areas.

In Boston, Royal Cloyd happened to go on a businessmen's tour of city neighborhoods: that changed his life and the future of a 616-acre area of endangered

This Queen Ann shingle and brick house was discovered by Bob Griggs when driving through Inman Park on his way to an appointment. At that time, Inman Park was a derelict neighborhood of run-down rooming houses whose yards were filled with junk cars and broken refrigerators. Bob's purchase and renovation of this house was the catalyst for the revival of the area. Recognizing the need to attract people and gain publicity for the renovation in progress, Bob started the annual two-day Inman Park Festival, which has become an Atlanta tradition.

Robert Griggs' dining room shows some of the intricate woodwork which is prevalent throughout the house.

nineteenth-century homes. When the bus stopped in the oval of Victorian houses called Union Park, Cloyd got out and let the tour proceed without him. He stood entranced with the inherent grandeur of the neglected homes falling to ruin around the once-handsome park. He decided to buy one of the five-story row houses, but it took considerable determination and some influence to get a mortgage in an area that had been written off by lending institutions since the panic of 1873! He subsequently learned that the city had been systematically razing South End houses at the rate of two per day in an attempt to wipe out its Skid Row.

The Cloyds moved into their house and began restoration. Within several months, a newspaper article illustrated some of the spectacular features of their home, while marveling at the nerve of the couple who dared to invest and move into the South End. There was an immediate flood of responses, and as a result of this publicity, a number of other families purchased houses and moved into the neighborhood. A further influx of homeowners arrived after Cloyd appeared on a television interview program. A large Christmas party in their huge double parlor attracted more interest. Among those attending was real estate broker Betty Gibson, who subsequently bought a house for herself and set up her office in the South End.

As revival proceeded, demolition was halted. Eventually the viability of the area was so well established that Cloyd was asked by the mayor to found a Boston Center for the Arts in the South End. This center was to be located in a wildly disparate collection of adjacent buildings, including a gasoline station, a piano factory, an old vaudeville theater, and a large circular structure built to house a Civil War cyclorama painting. The center established in these recycled buildings and opened with political fanfare was a tremendous additional asset for the reviving neighborhood.

In St. Louis, another large group of splendid mansions on the brink of extinction was rescued at the eleventh hour and brought back to useful life under similar circumstances; and a doomed neighborhood was saved in an incredibly short time through the same sort of follow-the-leader fashion. Slated for demolition to make way for an expressway, the homes surrounding Lafayette Park were in appalling condition, and the area was considered so dangerous that St. Louisans were afraid to set foot in it. By chance, young Tim Conley was driving past one day and stopped to look at one of the dilapidated mansions. Though a condemnation notice was posted on the facade, there were still sixty-two people living inside—eight of them in the drawing room alone, where half the ornate gilded ceiling had collapsed, exposing the joists. The handsome carved woodwork of the mantel had been painted purple, and the stairway ballisters were enameled orange, blue, purple, and brown. Nevertheless, Conley fell in love with the house and resolved to restore it. He bought it for $12,500 and persuaded the city to delay demolition for six months.

In that time, he had eighty-three truckloads of debris carted away, and installed new plumbing, wiring, and heating. He immediately repaired and painted the exterior, startling passersby, who stopped and stared in disbelief at the transformation. They were even more startled to see limousines bringing politicians and other guests to a party Conley gave. The stunning metamorphosis, heralded by newspapers and other publicity, encouraged others to buy homes on Lafayette Square. Within five years, two-thirds of the two hundred houses around the Square were being renovated, and buildings were selling within two or three days after being put on the market. House tours attracted ten thousand curious citizens, who lined up to gaze in amazement at the homes in this notoriously bad neighborhood.

The newly formed Lafayette Square Restoration Committee established a revolving fund with the aid of a loan from the National Trust for Historic Preservation to buy, repair, and resell buildings that were too far gone to attract purchasers. Meanwhile, crime in the area dropped 60 percent, and new stores and boutiques began opening. During all this time, the threat of an expressway through the park continued to hang over the community like the sword of Damocles. But meanwhile, through the efforts of new homeowners, Lafayette Square was designated a historic district and placed on the National Register, which precludes use of federal funds for demolition. And with a strong new constituency to fight the political battle, the expressway was finally defeated.

New Orleans's French Quarter and Baltimore's Fells

Point and Federal Hill are among the many communities that have suffered and survived the threat of an expressway, but one of the most noteworthy resolutions of such a problem was achieved in Brooklyn Heights. Robert Moses, New York City's powerful czar of parks, bridges, and highways, planned to build the six-lane Brooklyn-Queens Expressway diagonally across the fifty-block enclave of Brooklyn Heights that clearly would have wiped it out. Moses' will had never been successfully challenged as he rode roughshod over the built environment and people's lives while creating his remarkable empire, but now, for the first time, one of his roads was detoured.

Erected on a bluff overlooking New York harbor, the fine homes of Brooklyn Heights were built by distinguished nineteenth-century businessmen who found it easier to ferry across the East River to their homes than to travel by carriage from Wall Street all the way up to Greenwich Village. During the years of the Great Depression, the Heights suffered a decline, and a third of its homes were boarded up due to foreclosures. Later, bought up by absentee landlords, many of these homes were turned into shabby rooming houses, becoming a source of steadily spreading blight. However, throughout this sorry period, some of the older homeowners tenaciously hung on, and the Brooklyn Heights Association continued doggedly fighting for the improvement of the community even when it appeared past hope. The important point is that the association was still there when it was most needed. The Brooklyn Heights Association, founded in 1910, and the oldest such organization in the country, proved to be a vital tool in the fight against Moses.

After many fiery hearings and discarded alternative proposals, an ideal plan was formulated by engineer Ferdinand Nitardy, owner of one of the splendid old houses overlooking the waterfront. He proposed dividing the six-lane highway in half and setting it into the bluff on two levels. He and other homeowners volunteered to donate a portion of their gardens to cover over the expressway, creating a landscaped public promenade. Thus the expressway was completely hidden, and the promenade opened up the incomparable view of the harbor for the enjoyment of everyone. It has been dubbed by the American Institute of Architects' *Guide to New York* "one of the few brilliant solutions for the relation of automobile, pedestrian and city." And Brooklyn Heights, rescued by this plan, was designated the first New York City historic district when the Landmarks Commission was established in 1965.

Clearly, the efficacy of block and neighborhood associations can prove a major source of strength in surmounting urban problems. At the block level, much can be done to fight crime, improve sanitation, plant trees and flowers, and encourage neighbors to become acquainted and look out for their mutual interests. When block associations join together to form neighborhood associations, larger projects become possible, and political clout is available when needed.

As small an area as the four-square-block Stockade (named for the Dutch village founded there in 1661) in Schenectady, New York, has its Stockade Association, which sponsors an annual Walkabout, attracting visitors to tour its restored homes, each flying a flag from the period in American history when it was built. At the other extreme, the Lincoln Park Conservation Association represents seven contiguous neighborhoods bordering Chicago's Lake Michigan, comprising two square miles and 72,000 people. LPCA has a paid staff, publishes a newsletter, and undertakes code enforcement, area cleanup, youth activities, school improvements, and anything else of vital interest to residents, as well as working closely with city departments on behalf of the area.

Attractive community gardens have been created on unsightly, potentially dangerous vacant lots, bringing together volunteers to plant, weed, and water. Such activities have a dual benefit: not only beautifying the environment, but also increasing community pride. In Boston, the South End Federation of Citizens' Organizations devised a clever idea for cleaning up their streets, inventing a contest, ridiculously easy to win, in which the prizes were new garbage cans. Similar schemes have involved the planting of window boxes. Whenever destructive children can be persuaded to participate in such projects, their attitudes can be changed and their energies channeled constructively.

If neighborhood associations provide the strongest influence for effecting change, house tours are by far their most useful tool. People are invariably curious to see how others live, so it is fairly easy to attract a crowd with a little publicity and signs posted in store windows. Sometimes those who come only out of curiosity are so favorably impressed that they are tempted to buy houses. In the Capitol Hill section of Washington in its early stages of revival, real estate broker Barbara Held (who had a home and office in Capitol Hill) sponsored a Houses-in-Process tour. The free tour began with punch served in the Held office, and vans were provided to take groups to visit a series of houses in varying stages of renovation, with owners on hand to answer questions. And of course, for those who were interested, listings were available of houses for sale in the neighborhood.

The resident real estate broker is an important asset in a reviving neighborhood. In addition to Barbara Held and Betty Gibson in Boston's South End, resident brokers played a significant role in the development of Bolton Hill, the first of many large renovation neighborhoods in Baltimore, and in Inman Park in Atlanta. Boerum Hill (some of these so-called "Hills" are as flat as pancakes) in Brooklyn was so thoroughly depressed and unpromising that no real estate broker would touch it. So one of the pioneer homeowners started his own agency. That, plus house tours, made the difference in Boerum Hill's revival.

Besides publicity and house tours, parties can sometimes

be used effectively. An investment banker, having just completed the first restoration of a house in the shabby King William area of San Antonio, offered his home as the site for a charity party, bringing many prosperous citizens to see the potential of houses in the vicinity. In the early days of the Park Slope renaissance in Brooklyn, bank officers who had been reluctant to provide mortgages were invited to a cocktail party in a beautifully restored home and, persuaded by the surroundings and the obvious respectability of co-hosting homeowners, finally loosened their pursestrings. Another Park Slope renovator, who was denied insurance on his museum-quality restored home because the neighborhood was not considered a good risk, established the Brownstone Agency, providing insurance coverage designed especially for resident property owners in renovation neighborhoods.

The attitude toward reuse of old buildings has altered markedly in the past decade. It is now so widely accepted nationwide that federal and local governments have recognized the value of promoting it, with some localities offering special programs in urban homesteading to save abandoned housing and revive declining neighborhoods. Pressured by preservation organizations, the federal government enacted legislation providing tax incentives for restoration of buildings listed on the National Register (though it only covers those with rental income).

Renovation of houses in depressed inner-city areas by individuals for their own use, often followed by professional developers, has become known as "gentrification," a term imported from England, which connotes an influx of the gentry, or well-to-do upper classes. This so-called gentrification has had a broad beneficial influence— improving housing, sharply reversing deterioration, strengthening adjacent commercial districts, and increasing the local tax base. But the inevitable displacement of low-income families living in buildings purchased for renovation has made gentrification a dirty word, implying abuse of the underprivileged poor by the privileged rich. In fact, "gentrifiers" are not rich, or they would not be moving into depressed areas. They are usually people of modest means who are often hard-pressed to finance the purchase and improvement of their homes, and in some instances, have themselves been displaced from more affluent neighborhods. Furthermore, while gentrification has unquestionably dislocated some poor residents, studies have shown that in many cases displacement was caused by decay of the housing stock, which eventually leads to abandonment, benefiting no one.

Even so, most "gentrifiers" are concerned about the problem, and in some cases (such as Manhattan's West 87th Street Block Association) new homeowners have invested considerable time and effort to rehabilitate housing for low-income families in their neighborhoods. Some larger, organized efforts to address this problem have been successfully implemented by the Pittsburgh History and Landmarks Foundation and the Savannah Landmark Rehabilitation Project, using federal rent-subsidy programs to support rentals for the poor in their renovated homes. And finally, some municipalities have launched programs providing abandoned houses for "sweat equity," turning over apartment buildings to tenants for co-oping and rehabilitation rather than demolition so that those in residence can remain in the community.

<table>
<tr><td>5</td><td># What Kind of House Suits Your Needs?</td></tr>
</table>

THE HOUSE you decide to buy and how you choose to design the space inside will depend on your taste and pocketbook. But before you make the decision, you must understand your own needs and the limitations of the house you buy. First you must take stock of your family's needs and life-style as well as your budget. The right house for one person may be the wrong house for another. And what is beautiful to look at may not be comfortable to live in.

What is the size of your family, and has it reached its limits? Do you need separate bedrooms for children or accommodations for overnight guests? If you have small children, you want their rooms close enough so that you can keep track of them, but at the same time they should be able to entertain friends without disturbing you. And what about access and storage for baby carriages and bicycles? On the other hand, children do not stay small forever, so you must plan for their future needs as well as your own. Here is a checklist of factors to consider:

1. Adequate and conveniently located baths
2. Adequate storage space

3. Privacy for every member of the family
4. Space for hobbies and family projects
5. Play space for children
6. Facilities for entertaining
7. Ease of maintenance
8. Flexibility for future growth or shrinkage of the family

Planning of baths, kitchens, and laundry equipment can make life either pleasant or difficult. A kitchen is an important personal consideration. For the family that is not food-oriented, a small kitchen can be perfectly adequate. But people who are interested in cooking and entertaining may spend a great deal of time in the kitchen and enjoy having company while they work. For them, the size and location of the kitchen and its relation to the dining space can be a vital factor in the successful planning of living areas.

Consider carefully where you want your laundry equipment. Some people want it in the cellar, others in the kitchen, and the latest trend is a preference for bedroom areas, nearest the source of dirty linens. However, if bedrooms are on the upper floor, consider the potential damage that a washer overflow could cause to the floor below.

Many people who have found space at a premium think they can never have too much. They may be captivated by the idea of living in a large, rambling Victorian or a four-story brownstone. Be realistic about how much space you really need. Cities are dirty: hauling cleaning equipment up stairs can be exhausting, and cleaning help may not always be available. If you do not plan to have rental apartments, select a house that is large enough for your needs, but not too large for convenient maintenance.

Though most of us tend to choose our homes on an emotional basis, because we like the staircase or the lovely marble mantel, you should think realistically about the kind of house that will work best for you. If you plan to create a whole new floor plan, do not pay a premium price for sound walls and architectural details that must be ripped out. There are plenty of houses without any—why not buy one of them and save the others for those who want to restore? If you want to restore, you must be sure that what is in good condition is in a location where you can use it. Far too many renovators have been enthralled by marble-topped sinks and lovely paneling only to find that they must be sacrificed to make a workable floor plan. If parquet floors or decorative ceilings are where a bath or kitchen must go or the position of walls must be changed, they will be destroyed in the process of renovation. When the condition of the house is wretched, with floors buckling and ceilings falling, a new floor plan is usually no more expensive than using the existing one and replacing all of the plaster and flooring.

Much can be done to alter the interior, but the exterior walls put limitations on what can be done inside. Although houses can sometimes be enlarged without destroying their character, most cities regulate the size of the house that can be put on a given lot, and getting permission to change the outside dimensions is often not worth the effort. It is sometimes possible to increase the usable space in attached row houses by building additional rooms on the roof or opening up cellar space by excavating the rear garden. This has become quite common in New York, resulting in some stunning designs with two-story rooms flooded with light from glass walls. Ask an architect if such plans are allowed by your building code. (See pages 89–91 for an example.)

When dealing with row houses, the smaller the house, the more restrictions there are in terms of the number of rooms and the over-all layout. A wide house will allow you to have two rooms across either the front or rear if you wish. A deeper house allows you to use the interior space for baths and kitchens without cutting the size of front and rear rooms. A house that is both wide and deep will accom-

A small sampling of the amazing variety of architecture in downtown Savannah.

modate on two floors the amount of space that would require three or four floors of a narrow, shallow house.

· POSSIBILITY OF RENTAL INCOME

Many people shrink from the thought of becoming landlords, of sharing their homes with tenants. However, renting part of your house has a great deal to recommend it. In
some cases it is quite possible to cover your entire monthly
operating costs with rental income—to live rent-free. Of
course, there are certain responsibilities and problems involved in being a landlord, but if your house is well
planned and the apartments are designed to give tenants
as desirable a place to live as you would want yourself, you
will find that you have relatively little to do to earn that
welcome extra income. In fact, it can enable you to do
more with your own living space than you could ordinarily
afford. Whether you need or want rental income along

Double houses come in a variety of styles and can be found across the country: San Francisco (above, facing page), Savannah (below, facing page), and New Orleans French Quarter (above).

with the amount of space you need for yourself should determine the size house you buy.

A major consideration in creating apartments is privacy for your tenants as well as for yourself. Therefore, the most obvious location for rental units is in a garage or carriage house. Often large freestanding houses can be successfully divided into several separate living spaces (if city regulations permit), though it sometimes requires designing skill to do so without destroying the character of the house. Because floor plans of freestanding houses vary tremendously, it is not feasible to present plans here that would be applicable in a meaningful number of cases. Most renovators need the help of an architect in planning the conversion of a single-family home, and if you are thinking of incorporating rental units, it is advisable to have an architect look at the house before you make a commitment to buy it.

The plans illustrated here use row houses as examples because their layouts and built-in separate entrances are fairly standard. The same concept can easily be adapted to a raised cottage, and studying these plans may help you to look at and consider the possibilities for rental in whatever type of house you intend to buy.

· HOW TO WORK WITH SPACE

Your budget is the main limitation on what you can do with the space inside the house. Generally speaking, the more you can use of the existing house, the less expensive the renovation. Skimping on basics such as plumbing, heating, and wiring is never wise, but it is often possible to save money by avoiding floor-plan changes. Take for example this floor plan of a two-story San Francisco Victorian house shown on the opposite page. As a private residence the house can remain essentially as it exists. Any modernization can be done within the existing plan, holding renovation costs to a minimum. However, when rental units are

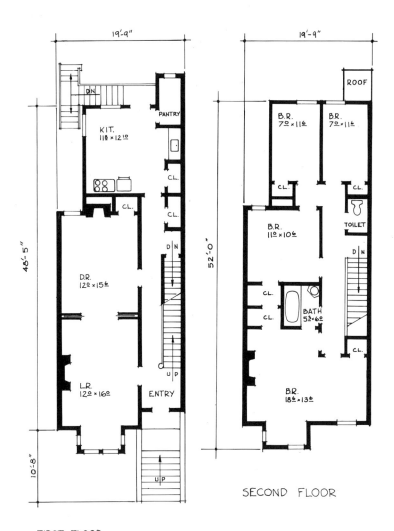

19'-9"

48'-5"

10'-8"

DN

PANTRY

KIT.
11⁸ × 12¹⁰

CL.

CL.

CL.

D N

D.R.
12⁰ × 15⁴

L.R.
12⁰ × 16⁰

ENTRY

U P

U P

FIRST FLOOR

19'-9"

52'-0"

ROOF

B.R.
7⁰ × 11⁵

B.R.
7⁰ × 11⁵

CL.

CL.

TOILET

B.R.
11⁰ × 10⁵

CL.

CL.

BATH
5³ × 6⁰

D N

CL.

B.R.
18⁵ × 13⁵

SECOND FLOOR

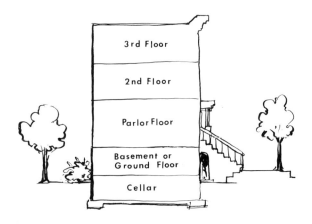

Cross section of typical high-stooped house.

to be created, the floor plan must usually be altered. The amount of alteration will depend on the number of apartments being created.

Using a row house floor plan as an example, the simplest conversion is the creation of a two-family house. A house with a high stoop makes an ideal two-family house because there are already two separate entrances, one under the stoop and another at the top of the stoop. The house merely has to be divided at the appropriate place to separate the two apartments. One apartment can be made on the ground floor by closing off or removing the interior stair between the ground floor and the one above, leaving the remainder of the house as a second apartment. Should access to the garden be required for the upper apartment, an exterior stairway can be added at the rear of the building. The only interior change necessary to complete the conversion is the addition of kitchens and baths for both apartments.

If the house has more than two stories, a two-story apartment can be created on the lower two floors. This is easily accomplished in a high-stooped house where the staircase is on the same side as the front door. The main staircase

Circular iron stairway in this Park Slope, Brooklyn, garden shows how parlor floor may have access to garden when ground floor is rented as an apartment.

can be used as an interior stairway for the lower two floors by erecting a partition beside the stair on the parlor floor to divide the lower and upper apartments. If the house has three stories, the lower two floors would become one apartment, and the third floor would be a single floor-through apartment. In a four-story house, two apartments would be created: one on the lower two floors and another on the upper two floors. In a five-story house, there would be a lower two-story apartment and an upper three-story apartment.

Instead of large two- and three-story apartments, you can create an apartment on each floor, or two apartments on each floor if the house is large enough to accommodate two baths and two kitchens on a floor. Or of course, you can have any combination of the above.

Though there is more income potential from two smaller apartments than one large one, there is likely to be more turnover in tenants, and the initial investment will be greater in terms of additional kitchens and baths and the necessary alteration of existing floor plans.

Since the upper floors were originally bedrooms,* it is usually fairly easy to create a two- or three-story apartment on the upper floors of a four- or five-story house. The pages following show the original plan (page 89) of the top two floors of a four-story house and the plans for two different renovations. Renovation Plan 1 (page 90) shows a simple conversion into a two-story apartment. Renovation Plan 2 (page 91) shows the same two floors made into two floor-through apartments. As you can see, the renovation for a two-story apartment required far less wall change and was therefore relatively inexpensive. The floor-through apartments cost substantially more.

However, floor-through apartments and studios can be created without gutting by clever use of existing space, provided that the condition of most walls, ceilings, and floors is good. If all ceilings and walls must be replaced, it will cost very little more to remove the studs and put up new partitions.

---

*When these houses were built, families had more children and several live-in servants. Since most of us no longer have a dozen offspring, and electrical appliances have greatly reduced the need for servants, the average nineteenth-century house is often larger than a single twentieth-century family needs.

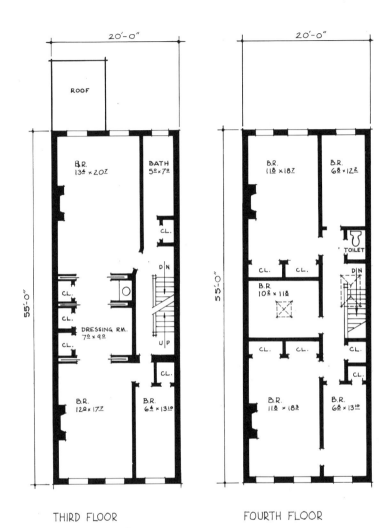

20'-0"

ROOF

B.R.
13⁴ × 20⁷

BATH
5⁰×7⁰

CL.

55'-0"

CL.

CL.

DRESSING RM.
7⁰ × 9⁰

CL.

D N

U P

CL.

B.R.
12⁰×17⁷

B.R.
6⁴ × 13¹⁰

THIRD FLOOR

20'-0"

B.R.
11⁸ × 18⁷

B.R.
6⁸ × 12⁷

TOILET

55'-0"

CL.

CL.

B.R.
10³ × 11⁸

D N

CL.

CL.

CL.

CL.

CL.

B.R.
11⁸ × 18³

B.R.
6⁸ × 13¹⁰

FOURTH FLOOR

89

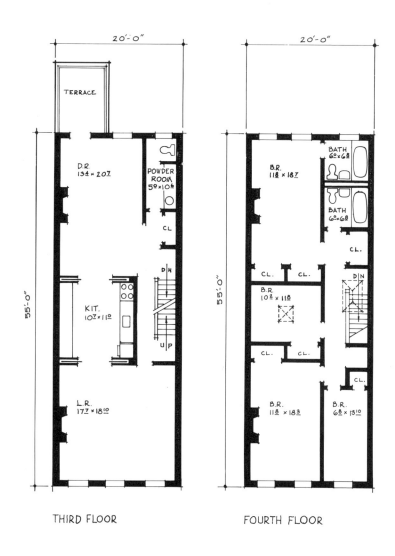

20'-0"

TERRACE

D.R.
13⁴ × 20⁷

POWDER
ROOM
5⁰ × 10⁴

CL

KIT.
10⁷ × 11⁰

D N

U P

L.R.
17⁷ × 18¹⁰

55'-0"

THIRD FLOOR

20'-0"

B.R.
11⁸ × 18⁷

BATH
6⁰ × 6⁸

BATH
6⁰ × 6⁸

CL.

CL.   CL.

B.R.
10⁴ × 11⁸

D N

CL.   CL.

CL.

B.R.
11⁸ × 18³

B.R.
6⁸ × 13¹⁰

55'-0"

FOURTH FLOOR

Renovation Plan 1 (one apartment)
By knocking out a few walls on the third floor, combining two
dressing rooms to make a kitchen, and dividing a bedroom on the
fourth floor to create two baths, these two floors became a spacious
duplex apartment for a family with two active boys.

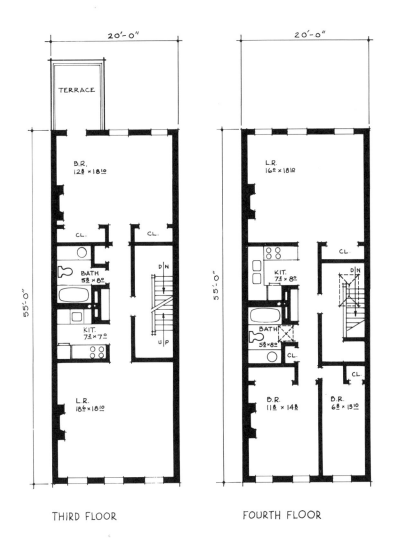

20'-0"

TERRACE

B.R.
12⁸ × 18¹⁰

CL.

CL.

BATH
5⁸ × 8⁰

D N

KIT.
7⁵ × 7⁰

U P

L.R.
18⁶ × 18¹⁰

55'-0"

20'-0"

L.R.
16⁰ × 18¹⁰

CL.

KIT.
7⁵ × 8⁰

D N

BATH
5⁹ × 8⁰

CL.

CL.

B.R.
11⁸ × 14⁸

B.R.
6⁹ × 13¹⁰

55'-0"

THIRD FLOOR

FOURTH FLOOR

Renovation Plan 2 (two apartments)
An almost total gutting was required to create two floor-through
apartments. Only the two bedrooms on the fourth floor remained
intact.

City regulations sometimes limit the number of dwelling units permissible in a building. Be sure to find out before you buy the house whether your plans for it are feasible.

If you plan to create rental apartments within a multistory house, you must weigh the pros and cons of lower versus upper for location of your own living quarters. The lower floors would seem to have every advantage—a minimum of stairs to climb and access to garden and cellar. But there are disadvantages. The lower floors are much darker, and ground floor ceilings in many houses are low. If the house has a high stoop, floor space required for halls across the front on the first and second floors must be subtracted from the lower apartment. Many houses have rear extensions that provide additional space: some are only one or two stories, while others go up the entire height of the house.

The upper floors have an abundance of light and lose no space across the front for hallways. If there is a rear extension that does not extend to the full height of the building, its roof can become a terrace for the upper apartment; or a large roof garden can be created on top of the house if the roof is flat.

Imagination can convert drawbacks into assets, whether you are dealing with a five-story row house or a Carpenter Gothic cottage. Removing all unnecessary partitions can increase the flow of light, making low ceilings appear higher. Properly scaled furniture makes a small room seem larger.

There is no such thing as a perfect house: there are spatial and financial limitations, as well as those imposed by city regulations. The most successful houses are those whose renovators have recognized the limitations, creating an environment that works for them within that framework.

6 | Finding a House

THERE IS NO right or wrong way to find a house; some people buy the first or second house they see, and others have to look for a year or more. Buying a house depends in part on your frame of mind—your willingness to make the commitment—partly on your diligence, and sometimes on just plain luck.

Driving around your city is a good way to become acquainted with various neighborhoods you may never have considered. Wherever there are old houses, there is a potential for renovation. If a neighborhood interests you, get out of the car and walk around. (You may even spot a "For Sale" sign.) Do not be afraid to talk to people and ask questions. You can even ring the doorbell of a house that has obviously been renovated. A renovator is usually friendly and eager to have others follow his example—and he may know of nearby houses for sale.

If a house appeals to you from the outside, try contacting the owner to see if he wants to sell. His name and address are listed under the property address in tax assessment books open to the public at the tax assessor's office. This is a long shot, but worth the try.

City house hunters must have the imagination to see the potential underneath the neglect, abuse, and additions that violate the original design. This derelict was restored to a charming brick colonial in Philadelphia's Society Hill.

You may even find a house by accident—like the Brooklyn couple who rang the wrong bell by mistake and found themselves talking to a family who had just decided to sell. They went through the house and liked it; the price was the lowest they had found in that neighborhood, and they agreed to buy on the spot.

But the obvious place to look for a house is in the classified section of the newspaper, where owners and real estate brokers advertise properties for sale.

· REAL ESTATE BROKERS

Real estate brokers must be licensed in the state in which they operate. Each person who acts as an agent for real estate (for management, renting, or selling) must have a license, either as a broker or as a salesman employed by a licensed broker.

A real estate broker (or agent) has one big advantage to offer the home buyer: He has listings for property that owners want to sell. It is far easier to find a house through a broker or his advertisement in the paper than trying to contact the owners directly.

Many people do not like the idea of using a broker because he receives a commission for his service which, although paid by the seller, is obviously included in the price of the house. However, if the broker finds you the right house, he will have provided a valuable service, and you should not begrudge him his fee. Can you imagine how difficult it would be to buy and sell property if there were no real estate brokers?

The broker acts as a third party between the buyer and seller, and his abilities as a negotiator are important. The broker is obviously interested in getting the highest possible price, because his commission is based on the sale price; but more important, he is interested in making the sale and will negotiate on your behalf in order to consummate the sale. The size of real estate commissions, usually based on a percentage of the sale price, may vary. Most cities have a standard rate, but this has been challenged by the federal government as price fixing. In addition to regular real estate brokers, discount brokerage firms have come into existence. Like discount stock brokers, they charge a lower commission because they provide less service with fewer frills.

In buying through a broker, you can avoid contact with the owner, perhaps preventing embarrassing moments as well as saving money. Most of us are not good bargainers, and we often find it difficult to ask an owner to lower his price or take less cash. And in buying an old, run-down house, you could be dealing with an absentee landlord whom you may find offensive. If you should happen not to like the broker, grin and bear it—you are buying a house, not a real estate broker.

The more brokers you deal with, the more you will learn. (*Never* hesitate to ask brokers, or any other professionals you may deal with, to explain technical terms you do not fully understand.) But there are times when dealing with one agent exclusively makes the most sense. How you go about locating a house to buy should, in large part, be determined by local practice. In some areas (such as New York City) there is absolutely no cooperation between real estate firms. Some properties are listed exclusively with one broker and can be purchased only through that broker. In the case of properties that are not exclusive, the competition is so fierce that advertisements will not give addresses for fear of giving away information to other brokers. In this situation, limiting yourself to one broker will prevent your seeing all the houses that are available. However, if you are shown a property by one broker and later buy that same property through another broker, the first broker is also entitled to a commission, for which you can be held liable. To avoid having to pay a double commission, always inform the second broker that you have already seen the house and cannot buy it from him.

In areas where there are Multiple Listing Services supported by most real estate firms, the common practice is to choose a broker and let him find you a house. Because each agent has access to all the houses listed in the service, the agent you choose can concentrate on getting to know your needs and spend the necessary time finding the right house for you. Needless to say, if you are going to deal with only one agent, it is important to pick the right one. In selecting an agent, remember that you are looking for a knowledgeble real estate person with whom you can communicate and work well. It doesn't hurt to talk to several different people before deciding.

- ### THINGS TO CONSIDER WHEN SELECTING A BROKER

1. Is he familiar with the neighborhoods in which you are interested? If you want to live in the middle of town, don't choose an agent who deals almost exclusively in suburban real estate.
2. Does he deal in property in your price range? If your budget is small and his average sale is much larger, find another broker.
3. If you are looking for an old house, an agent who sells only new houses is the wrong choice because the two of you will have different perspectives.
4. If you are looking for a derelict house to restore, be sure your agent understands this and is aware of the costs and problems of renovation. This doesn't mean that an agent has to be an expert on renovation, but beware if he seems to be making wildly unrealistic estimates of costs or problems of repair.

To get the most out of a broker or any professional, you must understand how to work with him. Tell him exactly what your needs are and what you can afford. And do not waste his time. Too many people spend Sunday afternoons looking at houses they have no intention of buying. On the other hand, a real estate broker may insist on showing you countless houses that are not what you are looking for. If this happens to you, tell him what you do not like about the houses and what you want instead. If he persists, find another broker. But you must be realistic: if you expect an elegant mansion for the price of a run-down rooming house, brokers will avoid you like the plague.

Do not be too upset if you catch a broker in a misstatement of fact. Much of the information he gives you was given to him by the seller, and very few brokers have time to check all the data on each property listed with them. Also, many brokers feel they will lose a sale if they admit that they do not know the answer to a question, and will make a stab at an answer. In every case, LET THE BUYER BEWARE—whether he is dealing with a broker or an owner—and check all critical information before agreeing to buy.

Besides finding you a house, there are two other important things a broker can do for you. Once you have found a property you are seriously considering, he can provide you with a written list of sales of comparable houses in the area. (A service that may not be provided by discount brokers.) This is important information in determining how much to offer for a house. In addition, he can give assistance with financing. A good broker will have current information on mortgage interest rates, on which lenders are providing loans, and which lenders are the most promising sources of mortgages on the house you want to buy.

In working with a broker, be firm and straightforward at all times. Do not let him, or the seller, pressure you into a hasty decision by talk of another party who is interested in the property. It is far better to lose a good house than to buy and be sorry. And you should not sign anything until you consult a lawyer, preferably one recommended by someone other than your real estate broker. (See page 154, "Hiring a Lawyer.")

Real estate practices differ widely: in many states it is illegal for anyone but a lawyer to draw up a contract. In this situation, the contract of sale is written by an attorney after buyer and seller have reached an agreement on price and terms, with the broker acting as an intermediary. This is far safer if there are any contingencies involved. However, there are a number of places where it is common practice for the real estate broker to fill in a standard contract form to make an offer to a seller. These are legally binding documents which become contracts of sale when signed by both buyer and seller. Whenever a buyer makes an offer through an agent by signing this form, he is obligated to purchase under those conditions if the seller signs it with no amendments. The standard procedure is to make the offer without benefit of lawyer, and if the offer is accepted, it is too late to amend the document. It is *essential* to get legal advice before signing a contract. Ask for a copy of your broker's standard form in advance of looking at any property. You can then show the form to your lawyer and discuss any parts that should be deleted or added when and if an offer is made. This will speed up the process once a house is found.

Asking for a small deposit (sometimes called "earnest money") as a *binder* on a particular property in which the buyer has serious interest is common practice with real estate brokers in some areas. This deposit is made before negotiation for purchase is begun in earnest, and is sometimes accompanied by the signing of an agreement. This practice is a means of determining the intent of the buyer and is proof to the seller of serious interest.

It is advisable to discuss earnest money binders with your lawyer in advance so that you will understand the local practice and how to handle the situation when and if you are faced with it.

Earnest money should have no meaning other than to prove your intent to enter into serious negotiations for purchase, so be sure this is made perfectly clear to the broker when the deposit is made—and make certain your contract specifies the money will be returned if no sale agreement is reached. Make a notation on your check that it is earnest money. And never give a deposit to an unlicensed broker; if you do, you can probably kiss the money good-bye. If you are asked to sign anything, be sure you read every word—and it is best to have your lawyer read it first. If what you are asked to sign is unclear, do not sign it. It's better to be safe than sorry.

Besides selling you a house, real estate brokers may be able to offer help in obtaining financing and insurance. Since many sales are conditional on a new mortgage, brokers develop business relationships with lenders. Do not rely on a broker to get you a mortgage, but do not refuse his help if he offers it. In many cities, real estate brokers double as insurance agents. They can give you information about kinds and cost of insurance and write a policy for you if you wish. But it generally pays to check with another insurance agent too.

• PROPERTY AUCTIONS

Property is auctioned for various reasons, one of which is a foreclosure sale brought about by the owner's failure to make mortgage payments or pay real estate taxes. A foreclosure sale may have complex legal problems because of the debts the property has incurred. And purchase at auction by a novice under any circumstances has potential dangers.

If you are interested in a property auction, discuss it with your lawyer so that you will understand all the problems involved. Property auctions can offer good opportunities to those who know what they are looking for.

Property auctions are advertised, usually a week or more in advance. Advertisements appear in legal and real estate publications as well as in local newspapers. A lawyer or real estate broker should be able to tell you where to find these advertisments.

Some cities offer a program called Urban Homesteading, or Sweat Equity. Under this program, houses foreclosed by the city may be purchased for as little as one dollar by people who can prove that they are willing and able to renovate and who guarantee to live in them for a specified time period. Check with your city Housing Department to find out if such a program exists in your area.

· HOUSE MOVING

It is possible to obtain a house for little or no money if you are willing to move it to your own lot. Such houses, often with historic pedigrees, have usually been rescued from demolition by preservation-minded citizens or organizations, provided they are removed from their sites, which are slated for other usage. Also, house-moving companies sometimes buy houses that are to be demolished for new construction. These houses are sold for a fixed price which includes moving them to your lot.

Moving a house is a complicated and costly procedure. It involves permits from state and city departments and approval from electric and telephone companies because of overhead wires. The site must be prepared as if a new house were being built: clearing land, pouring foundations, providing water and sewer connections, and bringing in electrical service. Once the house is set on the new foundations, there is still work to be done. How much will depend on the condition the house was in, and the damage that occurred because of the move.

If you are considering moving a house, take time to learn all that is involved, talking to people who have done it, if possible. And by all means, thoroughly check the company that will be moving the house. (See "Selecting a Contractor," page 252.)

A few words of warning before you begin the search for a house. The real estate business has its share of unscrupulous people. Owners and brokers have been known to deliberately lie about facts, causing unsuspecting buyers untold hardships. Then there are speculators who take advantage of inexperienced buyers by selling them houses at greatly inflated prices. There is no better protection against them than knowledge.

Mark and Walter Lowrey's perceptiveness made possible this incredible transformation of a New Orleans French Quarter ruin.

<table>
<tr>
<td>7</td>
<td># Is It a Good Buy and Can You Afford It?</td>
</tr>
</table>

BEFORE LOOKING at a single piece of property, you should make a thorough analysis of your own finances. The two most important questions to ask are:

1. How much cash do you have?
2. How much can you afford to pay each month for your living quarters (henceforth called rent)?

The amount of cash you have will determine the amount of financing you will need, and the amount of rent you can pay (along with rental income if there is any) will determine whether you can pay to operate the house. You may be able to purchase and operate the house as it exists when you buy it, but if you cannot pay for the necessary renovation or meet the expenses of the house after it is finished, you are in real trouble.

People usually know whether they like a house or not, but most do not understand how to evaluate anything beyond the purchase price. Any house you plan to buy must be evaluated in terms of your own needs and your ability to pay for it. A house should be a pleasure, not a financial burden. Renovation should be a creative adventure, not a nightmare. Knowing your financial limitations and the realities of purchase and renovation can bring you the rewards of a successful accomplishment as well as a sound investment.

Following is a list of factors to take into account when evaluating what you can afford:

1. The price of the house
2. The cost of construction
3. The cost of professional services (lawyer, architect, etc.)
4. The cost of carrying the house while work is being done
5. How the purchase and renovation will be paid for
6. The cost of operating the house when it is completed

Far too many people think that a low purchase price means a bargain. However, the purchase price must be assessed in light of the finished cost of the house, because the finished cost will determine whether the house is a good investment for you.

As an example, take two houses of the same size—one priced at $20,000 and the other at $50,000. To the novice, the $20,000 house would seem like the better buy. But if the $20,000 house costs $50,000 to renovate, is it still a bargain? If the $50,000 house will cost $10,000 to renovate, it will be a better buy than the cheaper one.

The cost of renovation is not limited to the price paid for the work. The cost of professional services, carrying costs (operating costs of the house while work is being done), and other expenses must be added to renovation costs to determine the cost of the finished house.

You must also consider how the renovation will be paid for. Financing must be obtained for the difference between the final cost of the property and the amount of cash you have. The availability of financing can also make a more expensive house a better buy than a cheaper one.

Lastly, you must estimate the operating costs of the house to determine whether you can afford to live in it. On a single-family house, the rent you can pay must cover all operating costs. If the house has rental apartments, the money you receive from them will help pay operating costs. If you are particularly astute in the house you buy and the renovation you plan, it is possible for rental income from tenants to pay all operating costs, allowing you to live rent-free.

All of these items will be discussed in detail later in this chapter, with forms given for calculating the costs of buying, renovating, and operating a house. However, before you even look at houses, it is possible for you to do some rough calculations of what you can afford.

Start your evaluation with the cost of operating the finished house. The operating costs that you will have to pay are as follows:

1. Mortgage payments
2. Real estate taxes
3. Heat/air conditioning
4. Electricity
5. Water and sewer charges
6. Insurance
7. Maintenance and repairs

• How to Calculate Monthly Mortgage Payments

Unless you have a substantial cash investment in your house, mortgage payments are usually the largest single operating cost (though utility rates have risen so steeply that they may now equal or exceed interest payments on some mortgages). To calculate the monthly payment on a given mortgage, you must know the interest rate and term. (The prevailing interest rate can be obtained by calling your bank and the term is the number of years you have to repay the mortgage debt.) Because interest is compounded, you cannot simply add 1% to the monthly payment on a 12% mortgage to find out what the payment would be if the interest rate were 13%.

If the mortgage is self-amortizing with equal monthly payments, you can use the table below to calculate the constant payment on mortgages with terms of 15, 20, 25, 30, and 40 years which have interest rates of 10%, 11%, 12%, 13%, 14%, 15%, 16%, 17%, and 18%.

This table expresses the constant annual payment as a percentage of the original amount of the mortgage. Thus a 15-year mortgage at 8% interest would have an annual constant payment of 11.47% of the original amount of the mortgage, whereas the same mortgage at 9% interest would have an annual constant payment of 12.18%.

To calculate the annual payment on any mortgage, take the appropriate percentage from the table and multiply the amount of the mortgage by that figure. Divided by 12 to get the monthly payment.

Constant Annual Percentage Table

Interest Rate	15 years	20 years	25 years	30 years	35 years	40 years
8%	11.47%	10.04%	9.27%	8.81%	8.53%	8.35%
9%	12.18%	10.80%	10.08%	9.66%	9.41%	9.26%
10%	12.90%	11.59%	10.91%	10.54%	10.32%	10.19%
11%	13.64%	12.39%	11.77%	11.43%	11.25%	11.11%
12%	14.41%	13.22%	12.64%	12.35%	12.19%	12.11%
13%	15.19%	14.06%	13.54%	13.28%	13.15%	13.08%
14%	15.99%	14.93%	14.45%	14.22%	14.11%	14.06%
15%	16.80%	15.81%	15.37%	15.18%	15.09%	15.04%
16%	17.63%	16.70%	16.31%	16.14%	16.07%	16.03%
17%	18.47%	17.61%	17.26%	17.11%	.17.05%	17.02%
18%	19.33%	18.52%	18.21%	18.09%	18.04%	18.02%

• OTHER OPERATING COSTS

Until you have a specific property in mind you will have to make some assumptions on operating costs other than mortgage payments.

Let us assume that you have a $25,000 income and can afford to pay 25% of it in rent—that gives you $6,250 a year to operate a house. Let us further assume that annual operating costs other than mortgage payments will run as follows:

Real estate taxes:	$600	Utilities:	$360
Water and sewer:	$250	Insurance:	$500
Heat:	$600	Maintenance:	$600

These costs add up to $2,910 a year. Subtract this from the $6,250 you have allotted for operating costs, and you will have the amount left with which to make mortgage payments on a single-family house—$3,340. What kind of mortgage can you carry for this amount of money?

Assume that the prevailing interest rate is 11% and that 30-year mortgages are available. The Constant Annual Percentage Table on page 109 shows that annual payments on such a mortgage are 11.43% of the original amount of the mortgage. Your $3,340 represents 11.43% of the amount of the mortgage you can carry.

To calculate the amount of the mortgage that a given dollar amount will carry, you divide that amount by the appropriate constant annual percentage.

In the illustration given above, $3,340 ÷ .1143 = $29,221.34, which is the amount of the mortgage you can afford.

To determine the price of the house you can afford, add the amount of cash you have to the amount of the mortgage. If you have $5,000 in cash, you could afford a single-family house worth $34,221.34 in the above illustration ($29,221.34 in mortgaging plus $5,000 in cash).

Assume that this house could accommodate your space requirements and still leave room for a rental apartment. Your rent would then be reduced by the amount of rental income you receive from the tenant. If you were able to get $250 a month in rent, it would cost you only $270 a month to live in the house.

If you want a more expensive house, rental income will enable you to have it. Assuming that you have the same $5,000 and can pay the same $6,250 in rent, what price house could you afford if you had rental income of $250 a month?

Using the same operating costs, exclusive of mortgage payments, as before, you will have $6,340 a year for mortgage payments ($3,340 of your rent and $3,000 in rent from your tenant). At 11% interest for 30 years, this will pay for a mortgage of $55,468 ($6,340 ÷ .1143 = $55,468).

You can now afford a house worth $60,468.06 (55,468.06 in mortgaging plus $5,000 in cash). Thus rental income of $250 a month almost doubles the price of the house you can afford.

Using the procedure explained in the above example, you can determine what price house you can afford under various circumstances. You can determine the effect of varying terms, interest rates, and rental incomes. The knowledge thus gained will help you determine what you should be seeking when you begin looking for a house to purchase. Although these calculations are based on many assumptions, they are nonetheless valid because they give you a rough idea of what you can afford.

But remember, just because you can afford to carry a large mortgage does not mean that a bank will be willing to give it to you. Chapter 8 gives you information about various kinds of financing. Keep this information in mind when you begin looking at houses. And be sure to do a thorough financial evaluation of any house you are considering before you buy it.

• PRICES ARE RELATIVE

Prices are indeed relative. A price that may be low in one city may seem high in another. And rental income can make an expensive house inexpensive to live in. We have purposely avoided using prices whenever possible because they vary so widely and because yesterday's high price may sound like a bargain tomorrow.

The price of the finished house is important to you, but the price must be judged and evaluated in terms of your ability to pay for it—i.e., how much cash you must invest and how much it will cost you to live in the house. If a house meets your financial requirements and gives you the amount of space you need, it is a good investment.

Generally speaking, the house with a low cash investment and low rent to the owner-occupant is the best investment. This means that you can realize maximum property appreciation either through selling or refinancing without pricing yourself out of the real estate market.

Although few people contemplate selling a house when they buy it, you should think about resale when choosing a house and planning the renovation, because five years from now you may be offered a better job in another city or for some other reason want to move. Your buyer will be just as concerned as you are about how much cash he will need to purchase and how much it will cost him to live in the house he buys. Low operating cost to the owner will make the house attractive to a large number of people— and if your cash investment was low and the mortgaging long-term, you can make a profitable sale without requiring an unreasonably high cash payment from your buyer.

· EVALUATING A SPECIFIC HOUSE

When you have found a house you like, do not agree to buy it until you have evaluated the property. Following is the basic information you need for this purpose:

1. Address of the property
2. Width and depth of the lot
3. Width and depth of the house and approximate square footage
4. Number of stories, excluding cellar

5. Whether there is a cellar
6. The current use of the building and its legal classification (single-family, multiple dwelling, rooming house)
7. Whether the house is to be purchased with or without tenants
8. If purchased with tenants, the rental for each unit
9. The type of heat (steam, hot water, forced air) and the type of fuel (gas, oil, coal)
10. Real estate taxes
11. The current tax assessment (divided into land and total assessment) and the current tax rate
12. The water and sewer charges
13. The amount and kind of insurance on the property, and its cost
14. The existing mortgages on the property—the principal owed, date due, whether they are self-amortizing and if not the amount of the balloon payment, the interest rate, the amount and date of payments, conditions of prepayment, and if there is a subordination clause.
15. The asking price and cash required to purchase
16. The amount and terms of any mortage the owner plans to give (take back)

Insist that the broker or owner provide all this information before serious negotiations are started.

The asking price of the property should be assessed in terms of the market value of other houses in the area. This can be done by looking at other houses for sale, by talking to owners in the neighborhood, by checking past sales at the city recording office, or by asking your real estate agent to provide you with a list of comparable sales. You may also have a licensed real estate appraiser evaluate the house.

Remember that prices differ from area to area. What may seem absurdly low to the inexperienced buyer may in truth be a high price for the neighborhood. This is not to say that you should never buy when the price of the house is inflated. If the cost of the finished house makes sense, it does not hurt to pay a premium price for the property, particularly if the house cannot be purchased otherwise. However, a buyer armed with information about neighborhood prices can often bargain more successfully. It is upsetting to learn after the house has been purchased that it could have been bought for less money. No one likes to be a sucker.

Before you go any farther, do not fail to check the zoning regulations to make sure the house can be used for your intended purpose.

Tana and Eddie Galob owned a building in downtown Philadelphia that had been a bakery. They had an architect draw up exciting plans to convert it to a home only to learn that the zoning laws would not allow anything remotely approaching what they had in mind. They sold the bakery and bought a brownstone instead.

Hugh Patrick Feely, former executive director of Chicago's Lincoln Park Conservation Association, said that his office constantly received calls for help from people who had bought property only to find that zoning prevents them from doing what they had in mind. "If only they'd check zoning before they buy," says Feely. "I don't know what they think we can do to help them afterwards."

Another word of warning: Do not buy a house just because it seems to be a bargain. The Lee Murphys bought a New York brownstone primarily because of its bargain price. However, unlike most Manhattan houses, it had no cellar. The furnace was located in the front of the ground floor—space needed for their apartment. The Murphys planned to dig a partial cellar to house the heating equipment. They soon discovered why the house had no cellar; it was built on solid ledge rock. Abandoning the risky idea of blasting under the foundation, they finally got special permission for an addition on the rear of the house for the heating plant, thereby sacrificing half of their small garden. They are pleased with the results, but there is little doubt that the Murphys spent more than it would have cost to buy a house with a cellar in the first place.

• INSPECTING THE HOUSE

Do not take the word of either broker or owner concerning the condition of the house. They are interested in selling the property and have no obligation to point out its defects. The house should be checked first by you and then by someone technically qualified to evaluate its condition. Here are the things you can check for yourself:

1. Is there water in the cellar or signs of a water problem there? A wet cellar can be difficult to remedy, can prevent the use of the area for storage, and can lower the value of the renovated house.
2. If you plan to keep the existing plumbing, check to see that water lines are brass or copper. The water lines are the small pipes that run along the ceiling in the cellar and are often exposed in the bathrooms of old houses. Use a magnet and ice pick (or other sharp instrument) to determine the kind of pipe. A magnet will adhere to galvanized iron pipe but not to lead, brass, or copper; lead is soft and will dent and scratch easily when probed with an ice pick. Also be sure to check water pressure by turning on all faucets full force, leaving them on below while trying the ones on the top floor. (See pages 173–82 for a complete discussion of plumbing.)
3. How sturdy is the staircase? Does it sag badly? Although stairs can be jacked up to make them level, beware of a staircase with excessive sag, because severe sag can indicate structural problems associated with settling. Jump on the stairs to determine how solid they are.
4. Are there signs of recent water damage from a leaky roof or around windows or on exterior walls?

5. Are floors fairly level? Place a marble on the floors and see if it rolls.
6. Check the general condition of floors and ceilings. This is important only if you plan to salvage them.
7. Are the windows in good condition? Open and close each one if necessary.
8. Check the wiring. How many outlets in each room? Are overhead lights operated by switches or pull-chains? Ask to see the fuse box. Are there ample fuses in addition to adequate main service for the size of the house? If there are few outlets, pull-chains, and an inadequate number of fuses, you can assume that you will have substantial wiring to do. (See pages 182–94 for a complete discussion of wiring.)

If you still want to buy the house after inspecting it yourself, call in an expert to check it further. Most older houses do not have serious structural problems, but why take a chance? It is quite a shock to the renovator who has bought a house thinking that it only requires modernizing kitchen and baths to discover that the plumbing is worthless and the foundations are crumbling.

Occasionally real estate brokers or owners are unhappy when you suggest having the house professionally inspected. Do not let this reluctance deter you. The commitment you make when buying a house is not to be taken lightly. You should know what you are buying because you cannot take it back and demand a new one when you discover a defect later.

A professional inspection of the house can be done by a home inspection service, a licensed professional engineer, a reputable contractor, or an architect who is knowledgeable about the structure and mechanical systems. Inspection cost is nominal in relation to your investment and provides invaluable information. If it prevents you from buying a house that could be a disaster to your budget, the money has been well spent. If the inspection turns up no serious problems, you will be reassured in knowing what you are buying. You may be able to avoid paying for an inspection before you are sure you want to buy the house by making your offer to purchase conditional upon a subsequent inspection.

Home inspection services and professional engineers are usually listed in the Yellow Pages. The service they provide is generally the same: a complete inspection of the house from top to bottom, with a written report of the conditions found. However, your professional inspector should be familiar with old houses, and if he is to do the proper job, you must tell him what you plan to do with the house. For instance, if you plan to relocate all the plumbing, he will only need to check the pipes in the cellar and the main water and sewer connections. He should thoroughly inspect the heating system, the foundations and exterior walls, the roof, leaders, and gutters, the stairs, and the beams. The plumbing and wiring are important only if you plan to reuse them. It is a good idea to accompany him on his inspection to see that he does a thorough job, but do not get in his way. You will also learn a great deal that may be of value to you later.

Most professional inspectors use a standard checklist form as the basis of their report. This form lists every aspect of the house with a rating (excellent, good, and so on) to be checked by the inspector. Some inspectors use only this standard form for their report, and others supplement the form with a written report of their own. Sometimes the report will give suggestions for remedial work and may include estimates for the cost of this work. As with everything else, you should check on the estimates given. Inspection reports are usually received three days to a week after the inspection is made. If you should need the report sooner, so stipulate when you hire the professional. If you use an architect or contractor to make the inspection, ask him for a written report and pay him for the job so you are under no obligation to him.

Although the kind of report issued will vary in detail, every report will provide valuable information about the condition of the house. An evaluation by an expert is essential if you are to know how much work must be done. His written report will also give you an advantage when negotiating the purchase: being aware of flaws will put you in the best bargaining position.

If you are satisfied with the condition of the house, you should then estimate the cost of renovating and operating to see if you can afford to buy it.

· ESTIMATING RENOVATION COSTS

If you are satisfied with the condition of the property, it is time to think about the feasibility of renovating it. Without plans and specifications for the renovation, the best that even an expert could do is a "guess-timate" of construction costs. You could talk to an architect or contractor about the house and ask him what he thinks your job should cost. Renovation costs are often calculated on a price-per-square-foot basis and sometimes, when house sizes are fairly standard, as in row houses, on a cost-per-floor basis.

If you have friends who have done renovations, ask them about the cost of their jobs and compare their scope to the one you are planning. A call to a plumber, electrician, or other craftsman may give you rough prices of specific costs, and a visit to appliance dealers and lumber yards will acquaint you with prices of appliances and fixtures. Add 10–15% for contingencies to estimates in order to be realistic.

There are costs other than construction that must be included when figuring the cost of the finished house. Since lawyers are necessary when purchasing property and are often used for legal assistance in financing and other areas related to the house, their fee is part of the cost of the property. The same is true of architects, home inspection services, and closing cost of purchase and refinancing.

Carrying costs are seldom considered by renovators, and yet if the owner is not living in the house while the work is being done, he will have to pay to operate the house as well as the place where he is actually living. The longer the renovation takes, the higher the carrying costs. Carrying costs on a vacant house consist of the following:

1. Mortgage payments
2. Real estate taxes
3. Water and sewer charges
4. Electricity (needed for construction)
5. Heat (must be provided in winter to keep pipes from bursting)
6. Insurance

When the renovation is extensive and the owner does not move in until the work is complete, it is not unusual for a year to elapse before the house is occupied: six months for planning and obtaining necessary financing, six months for construction. In such cases, carrying costs can be substantial.

The following form shows what items to include in estimating the cost of completing a house:

PURCHASE AND RENOVATION SUMMARY FORM
___

Costs:

Purchase price of property:	$_____
Professional inspection fee:	$_____
Legal fees (purchase and refinancing):	$_____
Financing costs (points, mortgage broker's fee, etc.):	$_____
Closing costs (purchase and refinancing):	$_____
Tenant relocation costs:	$_____
Architectural fees:	$_____
Construction costs:	$_____
Contingency on construction:	$_____
Carrying costs (if not living in the house during construction):	$_____
Total Cost of the House:	$_____
Less owner's cash:	$_____
Amount of Financing Needed:	$_____

___

The Purchase and Renovation Summary Form is used to determine the cost of the finished house and the amount of financing the owner must obtain.

Financing costs (mortgage broker's fee, points, or discount on the mortgage) may be deducted from the amount of the mortgage and not paid directly by the owner. However, these costs will affect the amount of cash an owner must have. If the owner obtains a new mortgage of $40,000 from which $1,000 is deducted for financing costs, he will receive only $39,000. If he needed $40,000 in financing to accomplish the purchase and renovation, he will have to come up with an additional $1,000 in cash.

• ESTIMATING OPERATING COSTS ON THE FINISHED HOUSE

Once you have estimated the price of the finished house, you must determine whether you can afford to live in it. Use the following form to estimate operating costs and the amount of rent you will have to pay:

INCOME AND OPERATING SUMMARY FORM

Operating Costs:	Annually
Mortgage payments	
1st mortgage:	$_____
2nd mortgage:	$_____
Real estate taxes:	$_____
Water and sewer:	$_____
Heat:	$_____
Insurance:	$_____
Electricity:	$_____
Maintenance and repairs:	$_____
Total Operating Costs (including amortization):	$_____
Less rental income:	$_____
Cost of Owner's Apartment:	$_____

• *Mortgage Payments.* When you filled in the Purchase and Renovation Summary Form, you figured how much mortgaging you would need to buy and renovate the house. Now you will have to calculate the payments on this financing. If you can reasonably expect to get all the needed money from one mortgage, you can calculate the payments by using the Constant Annual Percentage Table on page 109. If you will need two mortgages, the term and interest rate may be different on the two, so you should calculate the payments separately. If the second mortgage is from the seller, you should know the interest rate he will charge and the term he will give.

• *Real Estate Taxes.* You can get this information from the owner. You should know the tax assessment and the current tax rate so you can calculate the amount yourself. This information should be checked at the tax assessor's office. There is a chance that your taxes will go up after you complete renovation. See Appendix, page 305, for a discussion of real estate taxes.

• *Water and Sewer Charges.* Sometimes this cost comes in the form of a tax paid once or twice a year, and sometimes the water is metered, with sewer charges based on water usage. The seller will be able to give you information on what these costs have been in the past. If you will have a different number of kitchens and baths, his costs should be adjusted to reflect the change. A call to the city water department will tell you how these charges are made.

• *Heat.* The seller will also be able to supply you with his past heating bills. Often heating costs are reduced when the house is renovated because all windows and doors are repaired and the house properly sealed. A call to a fuel supplier should give you an idea of the cost to heat a house the size of the one in question. And if the owner is unable or unwilling to supply you with his costs, you can call his fuel supplier to get last year's cost. See page 195 for a discussion of heating.

• *Insurance.* You can also get the cost of his insurance from the seller. However, his coverage might be insufficient based on the price you are paying and money you may be investing in improving the house. Be sure that the amount and kind of insurance is adequate for your needs. See Appendix, page 309, for a discussion of insurance.

• *Utilities.* The electricity and gas that your tenants use can be separately metered so they pay their own bills. However, you will have to pay for what you use and for any public areas. You can use the owner's past bills or call the utility company for an estimate of costs.

• *Maintenance and Repairs.* These bills should be minimal for at least five years if the house is completely renovated. However, you must make some allowance because there will always be minor problems such as a clogged toilet. And you must get in the habit of putting aside money for major items such as painting.

Once you have estimated operating costs, you must figure the amount of rental income you can expect before you know how much it will cost you to live in the house.

• RENTAL INCOME

If you are presently renting, you will have an idea of rents being charged in your city. However, there can be a wide variation in rents depending on location, apartment size, and other features. For the purpose of estimating how much it will cost you to live in the house, it is best to set rents at a reasonable rate, even though you may be able to get more—disaster may result from basing your purchase on unrealistic rental income.

If you are not familiar with the rental market, spend a day apartment hunting to acquaint yourself with the kinds of apartments available and the rents being charged. You should then be able to set realistic rents for your apartments.

• THE VALUE OF ESTIMATING OPERATING COSTS

Once you have filled out an estimated income and operating statement for the house you are interested in buying, you will know whether the cost to you falls within the rent you have set for yourself.

If the operating cost is too high, you must do one of the following:

1. Raise rents to cover costs above what you can afford to pay.
2. Reduce the amount of mortgaging by increasing your cash investment.
3. Reduce the amount of mortgaging by reducing the purchase price and/or the cost of construction.

Before and after: two houses in Philadelphia's Society Hill.

4. If you had planned on a single-family house, you can add a rental unit if allowed under local zoning laws.

All other costs are relatively stable, and reductions in them would be slight and not sufficient to make a meaningful reduction in operating costs.

If this economic evaluation shows that the project is within your budget (that you can afford to live in the house

with no more cash invested than you have available), you are ready to begin negotiations for purchase. If the house is beyond your budget, forget it and start looking again. If you were thinking of a private house, you may have to consider rental income to help defray the operating expenses. If you were planning only one rental unit, maybe you should consider a larger house to maximize income.

After doing an economic evaluation, you should know what needs to be negotiated in purchasing the house. The price may have to be reduced, or you may have to buy for less cash than is being asked. Perhaps the seller will have to provide some of the necessary financing.

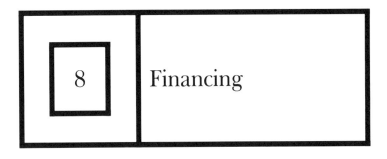

8 Financing

WHETHER YOU CAN AFFORD to buy, renovate, and live in your house without financial strain is the question you must ask when considering the purchase of a house for renovation. Yet the average home buyer knows little or nothing about the various kinds of mortgages available and how to evaluate his ability to pay for the house in terms of anything beyond the purchase price, which may be only a small part of the finished cost.

Did you know that a good mortgage is an asset, not a liability? That the terms on which you arrange to buy a house may be more important than the price? You must know all about mortgages before being able to determine whether you can afford to buy a house, and the best possible means of financing the purchase and renovation.

• HOW TO GET A MORTGAGE

The major sources of mortgage money are savings banks, savings and loan associations, building and loan associations, and FHA-approved lenders (mortgage bankers). Commercial banks occasionally make mortgage loans as a special service to customers. Insurance companies and some private individuals are also sources of mortgaging.

Phone calls to local banks (the term "bank" referring to all types of lending institutions) will give you an idea of their willingness to provide a mortgage. You can get additional information by personal visits to mortgage officers of the more receptive banks. Of course, no commitment for a mortgage will be made until an application is submitted.

You should learn all you can about the availability of mortgaging before you even begin to look for a house. Each bank has its own particular lending policy. Some put heavy emphasis on the borrower's income. Some are only interested in single-family homes, while others prefer income-producing property. The location of the property may be a critical factor.

Because getting a mortgage in an emerging neighborhood can be extremely difficult, the preferences of banks may be a factor in determining the house you buy. Some place a maximum limit on the amount they will lend regardless of the value of the property. Consider lending practices in your area when shopping for a house: the amount you can borrow from a bank will determine whether you will need additional financing to purchase and renovate a house.

When seeking a first mortgage, you should pull any strings that you can. If you have business, personal, or family connections in the banking world, use them. Leave no stone unturned. You want to get the best mortgage at the most favorable terms possible.

One Brooklyn couple had several discussions about mortgages with a large New York City bank. Not only was their application for a mortgage rejected, but in an arbitrary and high-handed manner. Shortly thereafter, the chairman of the board made a speech about bankers needing to recognize their responsibility to help solve urban problems. Irate, the couple wrote him a letter explaining how they had been treated by his bank. Within ten days the couple received a commitment from the bank for the mortgage they needed.

If mortgage money is difficult to obtain in your area, a mortgage broker may be the answer. A mortgage broker specializes in placing mortgages. He charges a fee for this service (usually a percentage of the amount of the mortgage), but you pay him nothing unless he obtains a mortgage for you.

The idea of paying someone to get you a mortgage may seem ridiculous until you find out how difficult it can be to obtain adequate financing. A mortgage broker keeps abreast of the mortgage market and has developed a relationship with many lenders. He knows what banks have mortgage money (including out-of-town banks that you would not know about), what kind of property they are interested in, and the best way to present your case. An application from a mortgage broker will often receive more favorable attention than the same application submitted by the owner, because the lender feels that he can rely on the broker to bring him a sound investment, whereas he knows nothing about the owner. (A mortgage broker would not stay in business long if many mortgages placed by him had to be foreclosed.)

Mortgage brokers are usually listed in the Yellow Pages under "Mortgages." Or you could ask your lawyer or real estate broker for the names of mortgage brokers who handle mortgages for the type of property you plan to buy. Your lawyer or real estate broker may also be able to help you find the mortgage you need.

• THE APPLICATION FOR A MORTGAGE

If you want a mortgage, you must submit an application first. It is sometimes better to apply to more than one bank so that hopefully you will have several mortgages from which to choose. However, when a mortgage application entails a fee (which is usually applied to closing costs and is forfeited if you do not accept the mortgage), submitting several mortgage applications can be costly. Processing a mortgage application can take time, so be sure to get yours in as soon as possible. A large mortgage is usually more difficult to obtain than a small one and frequently requires approval of a mortgage committee that does not meet often.

The more you know about your own finances, the kind of mortgage you need, and the particulars of the property to be mortgaged, the more receptive the mortgage officer and the bank will be to your application. Here is the kind of information most banks require:

1. A financial statement from you
2. Description of the property—location, size, number of apartments (if not a single-family house), rentals from each, estimate of operating costs (all of this on the finished house even if the house is yet to be renovated)
3. Description of renovation (with floor plans if the house is to be substantially changed) and estimate of the cost of the work, if the mortgage is to be based on the renovation

Be realistic in estimating rental income and operating costs, because the bank will adjust whatever they feel is inaccurate. (Lenders usually figure the former on the low side and the latter on the high side.) When estimating renovation costs, it is usually a good idea to pad them a little unless you have actual bids for the work—you will probably find the costs higher than you expected. On pages 120 and 121 you will find forms for estimating renovation cost and operating expenses. These will be helpful in presenting your case to the bank.

Ask the bank how long it will take to process your application. Then you must sit back and wait until you receive an answer. During the wait, keep your fingers crossed, rub your rabbit's foot or other good-luck charm, and pray for the best.

- THE IDEAL MORTGAGE

Ideally you want one mortgage to provide the entire amount of money you need to purchase and renovate your house. This mortgage must have payments you can meet without financial strain, and if it is not to be a burden to you at some future date, it should be transferable and have a prepayment clause.

If you need financing in order to purchase, you can obtain the mortgage before you buy, so that you will receive all or part of the money at the time you take title to the house. It can be obtained after you purchase, and placed on the house before renovation begins if you need money to pay for the renovation. And if you are lucky enough to have sufficient cash to pay for the house and renovation (but do not wish to tie up all this cash permanently in the house), you can wait until the renovation is complete to look for a new first mortgage. In this case, you are in an ideal situation: you will have time to shop around, and because the bank will be able to see the finished house, judging it on its own merits rather than from plans, you will probably be able to get a more favorable mortgage.

Because an ideal mortgage is often difficult to obtain, particularly in transitional neighborhoods, renovators can make their lives easier by fully understanding all the financing options open to them. If you have a limited amount of cash and want to make the most of it, this detailed mortgage primer may be helpful to you. Some of these financing options (now called "creative financing") are used in sales of all kinds of houses in any neighborhood when interest rates are exhorbitant or when money is very tight.

• A MORTGAGE PRIMER

A *mortgage* is a loan for which your house is the security. The amount that the lender *(mortgagee)* will give you is based on the value he could easily recoup on the market by selling the house if you *(mortgagor)* failed to meet your obligation and repay his loan. If you did fail to repay, he would have to go through the legal procedure of *foreclosure* in order to sell the house and recover his loan. The amount of the mortgage loan is called the *principal* and must be paid back by the end of the mortgage period. The *term* of the mortgage is the number of years you have to repay it.

• Self-Amortizing Mortgages

The most common type of mortgage is the *self-amortizing* (self-liquidating) mortgage, which has payments designed to repay the full debt over the term of the mortgage. The mortgage payments are made up of interest plus amortization. *Interest* (stated as a percentage of the debt) is the amount you pay to the lender for the use of his money. *Amortization* is the amount of the loan you repay yearly, thereby reducing the principal owed. Mortgage payments are normally made monthly and are based on the rate of interest and the amount of amortization to be paid. In self-amortizing fixed-rate mortgages, the term determines the amount of amortization. The longer the term, the more the amount can be spread out, and consequently, the lower the monthly payments. (However, the longer the term, the larger the amount of interest you will pay.) The following chart gives an example of monthly payments for varying terms, on a self-amortizing mortgage of $30,000 at varying interest rates:

Constant Monthly Payments on a $30,000 Mortgage

Interest Rate	15 years	20 years	25 years	30 years	40 years
8%	$286.70	$250.94	$231.55	$220.13	$208.60
9%	$304.29	$269.92	$251.76	$241.39	$231.41
10%	$322.39	$289.51	$272.62	$263.28	$254.75
11%	$340.98	$309.66	$294.04	$285.70	$278.49
12%	$360.06	$330.33	$315.97	$308.59	$302.56
13%	$379.58	$351.48	$338.36	$331.87	$326.86
14%	$399.53	$373.06	$361.13	$355.47	$351.35
15%	$419.88	$395.04	$384.25	$379.34	$375.97
16%	$440.62	$417.38	$407.67	$403.43	$400.70
17%	$461.71	$440.05	$431.34	$427.71	$425.50
18%	$483.13	$463.00	$455.23	$452.13	$450.36

In the early years of a mortgage you will be paying a larger amount of the monthly payments in interest, because interest is based on a percentage of the principal owed. As the principal is reduced, the amount of the interest is likewise reduced. The total monthly payment remains the same; but the ratio gradually changes so that in later years you pay less in interest and more in amortization. The following chart shows the breakdown of annual payments on a five-year $10,000 mortgage at 10% interest whose monthly payments are $212.50.

	Annual Interest	Annual Amortization	Principal Balance
1st year	$930	$1,620	$8,380
2nd year	$750	$1,800	$6,580
3rd year	$570	$1,980	$4,600
4th year	$370	$2,180	$2,420
5th year	$130	$2,420	—

The amortization payments represent your *equity* (or ownership) in the property. By the time the mortgage is fully amortized, you will own the house free and clear. Amortization can be considered as putting money into a forced savings account. If you should sell the property for the same price you paid for it, you will get back all amortization you have paid on your mortgage—whereas you get nothing back when paying rent on the place you live in.

A mortgage states all the conditions of the loan: year placed, amount borrowed, rate of interest, term, amount and date of payments, and other conditions. The mortgage is then recorded with the city and becomes a *lien* (claim) against the property. Mortgages are a matter of public record and can be checked at the city recording office. The mortgage debt is not automatically removed when the mortgage is paid off. In order to remove the mortgage a document (called a satisfaction piece) must be filed when the debt is paid.

- ADJUSTABLE RATE MORTGAGES

In a fixed-rate mortgage, the interest rate, and consequently the monthly payment, remains the same for the life of the loan. In an adjustable-rate mortgage (ARM) the interest rate fluctuates with market conditions. There are dozens of variations on the ARM, but basically the interest rate for each version is tied to a published government index of money rates, such as the treasury bill rate. Instead of remaining constant, your mortgage rate will change over the life of the loan. How often and under what conditions will be explained to you by the lender. The interest rate on some adjustable-rate mortgages can change as often as once a month; however, the monthly payments will remain the same for a specified period (anywhere from one to five years) before being adjusted to account for the over-all increase or drop in interest rates. If the interest rate has climbed during this period, the new amount due is added to the principal amount owed. Thus your loan balance can actually grow instead of decreasing. This is known as *negative amortization*. Some ARMs have limits on the amount of negative amortization that can accrue, and some have limits on how much interest will be allowed to fluctuate over the life of the loan.

Borrowers have been slow to accept the adjustable-rate mortgage for obvious reasons: they are very uncomfortable about not knowing the size of future monthly payments when taking on long-term responsibility for such payments. Lenders, however, tend to favor ARMs because interest rates that fluctuate with market conditions prevent their being locked into long-term, low-interest loans, as they have been in the past.

There is a decided risk to the borrower with an ARM. He has an advantage if interest rates fall: his mortgage payments will be lowered, whereas the payments on a fixed-rate mortgage will remain the same (higher than the market rate).

However, if interest rates rise, the person with the fixed-rate mortgage will be in a better position. Many lenders have recognized this problem and are offering a *convertible adjustable-rate mortgage*. A convertible ARM can be converted to a fixed-rate mortgage under terms specified by the lender, usually at the time of the first adjustment of the loan. The fixed interest rate will be based on a specified index. This would seem to allay some of the fears of the borrower by giving him the ability to change to a fixed-rate mortgage without having to incur the closing costs of refinancing. This, however, does not totally eliminate the risks of ARMs.

The latest twist in ARMs is the *graduated-payment adjustable-rate mortgage* (GPARM). Under this plan, the scheduled monthly payment at the beginning of the loan is insufficient to fully amortize the loan; in order to make up this shortfall, the monthly payment increases by a set amount each year, typically 7½% a year for the first five years. (This is in addition to adjustments that are made because of changes in interest rates). There is a similar fixed-rate loan called a *graduating equity mortgage* (GEM). The GEM monthly payment increases by a set amount each year, either until the loan is paid off or for a designated period, after which the payments level off for the remaining term.

Graduated payment mortgages are designed to make home ownership possible for a larger number of people. The assumption is that a person's income will rise sufficiently to be able to meet the increased payments. This kind of loan involves risk. Be sure you fully understand what you are committing to before taking on a graduated-payment loan, particularly a GPARM, where the interest rate on the mortgage may also rise.

• MORTGAGE BOND

A mortgage is attached to the property, not to the borrower. At the time the mortgage is placed, the lender requires the borrower to sign a mortgage bond, an instrument in which the borrower promises to pay off the mortgage debt. Bonds make the borrower personally responsible for the debt—which means that in the event of foreclosure, if the house is sold for less than the amount still owing, the borrower must make up the difference. (Personal responsibility for the mortgage debt can sometimes be avoided by the use of corporate ownership.) However, if the amount and conditions of the mortgage are favorable, a personal guarantee should not be a deterrent. The homeowner does not plan to allow the mortgage to be foreclosed because he would lose his house and destroy his credit rating.

• MORTGAGE CONDITIONS

The conditions of the mortgage are important to you. Your mortgage payments usually are the most expensive item in the operating cost of your house. In addition, the mortgage conditions may be important when and if you ever want to sell or refinance your house.

• *Transferability.* If the mortgage is transferable (assumable), it remains on the property even if it is sold, which means that the buyer can take over (assume) the mortgage. But if the mortgage contains a *due-on-sale clause,* the loan must be paid off when the property is sold. The buyer must either pay all cash for the house or raise money by getting a new mortgage on the property himself. Although the due-on-sale clause allows the lender to demand payment of the remaining amount of the loan, many lenders will allow the buyer to assume the loan if the interest rate is escalated to the prevailing market rate.

Some older mortgages that allow the loans to be transferred require lender approval of the buyer.

• *Prepayment Clause.* Ideally, you should be able to pay off your mortgage at any time before the end of its term, if you wish to. To assure this right, your mortgage should have a prepayment clause.

It costs the lender money to place the mortgage. He usually does not recover this cost until the mortgage has been in effect for several years. Therefore, some mortgages will not allow prepayment without an interest penalty. Some states limit a lender's right to prepayment penalties.

A large prepayment penalty can be a burden; but a small penalty (such as three months interest on the early payment) will not be an undue hardship. The real hardship can come from a long-term inability to repay without a large penalty. If you wish to sell, your buyer will be unable

138 · *Buying and Renovating a House in the City*

to raise cash by getting a new first mortgage himself unless he pays the penalty. And should you ever need cash, you will be unable to get a larger new mortgage to replace the reduced existing one unless you pay the penalty.

• *Interest Rate.* The interest rate is important only as it affects the operating cost of the house. A higher interest rate obviously increases the amount of the mortgage payments, thereby increasing operating costs. However, high interest rates alone should not prevent you from borrowing money. A house can be a good investment even with a high-interest mortgage; and if the mortgage contains a prepayment clause, it can later be refinanced favorably if the interest rate drops. In the meantime, you are paying off the mortgage and also stand the chance that the property will appreciate in value.

If, on the other hand, the interest rate on your mortgage is well below the current rate, you have a real asset. One young couple insisted that an old low-interest mortgage of $3,000 be removed before they took title to their house. They then had to borrow against securities they owned in order to finance the purchase and renovation. But they would have needed to borrow $3,000 *less* if they had left the existing mortgage; what they did, in effect, was to re-borrow the $3,000 at a higher interest rate.

If you have a low-interest mortgage on your house, the lender may be willing to refinance your loan on mutually advantageous terms. In order to remove a low-interest loan from his books, he may agree to increase the amount of the loan at a below-market rate. When Martha Stamm decided to move from New York to Atlanta, she talked to her bank about refinancing her house in order to free up some capital. The interest rate on her mortgage was several points below the prevailing rate. She explained to the bank that she was unwilling to pay the prevailing rate, and would take out a second mortgage instead of refinancing if they could not work with her. The bank agreed to increase the mortgage by 50% in return for a 1½% increase in the interest rate. It was a good deal for both parties.

• SECONDARY FINANCING

There is no limit to the number of mortgages that can be placed on a property. Mortgages are referred to as first, second, third, and so on, to designate their place in line as liens against the property. The first mortgage is called *primary financing* and is the first claim against the property in foreclosure; all subsequent mortgages are *secondary financing* and have subordinate claims in foreclosure—the first mortgagee must collect his debt in full before the second mortgagee can lay claim to the property, and so forth down the line. A second mortgage is thus subordinate to the first, and a third subordinate to the second as claims against the property. As you can easily see, there is more risk involved in holding a second mortgage than a first mortgage, because if a foreclosure sale does not bring in enough money to cover them both, the second mortgagee may be left holding the (empty) bag. For this reason, banks and other lending institutions generally place only first mortgages. Second mortgages are available from individuals or firms specializing in secondary financing.

The conservative mortgage policies of most lending institutions have denied inner-city homeowners the liberal terms and amounts available to suburban home buyers. This situation is in part understandable, because the decay that has infected many city neighborhoods has caused mortgagees to lose a great deal of money as property values declined. Nonetheless, this negative attitude has penalized city renovators and has made it difficult and sometimes impossible for them to obtain anything but minimum bank financing. For this reason, second mortgages are common to city property owners and have become a necessary means of financing for many renovators.

As a renovator, you must consider not only the financing

of the purchase, but the financing of the renovation as well. Therefore, it is doubly important to know how to get secondary financing under the most favorable terms.

• Discounting

Because secondary mortgaging involves a risk, it is usually more expensive financing than a first mortgage, with a *discount* (premium) charged by the lender. This discount is a percentage of the loan deducted from the principal at the time the money is borrowed; the loan is then repaid as if the borrower had received the full amount. Although second mortgages are generally written at the prevailing interest rate, the discount has the effect of raising the interest rate.

The amount of discount charged will vary according to the area and the availability of money. A second mortgage might be discounted at a rate of 5% a year, which means that a three-year mortgage would be discounted 15%. This means that on a $10,000 mortgage, the mortgagor would receive only $8,500 (or $10,000 minus 15%) but would pay interest on the full $10,000.

Second mortgages are often short-term loans, with terms of from three to five years. If a short-term mortgage were to be completely self-amortizing, the payments would be extremely high. Therefore, many second mortgages are not self-amortizing and have a large principal payment owed when the mortgage term is ended.

Consider the above mortgage of $10,000 at an interest rate of 10% plus an amortization rate of 4%—a total of 14% annual constant payment. In three years the borrower would have reduced the principal by only $1,324. Subtracted from the $10,000 debt, that leaves $8,676. Since he received only $8,500 from the lender to start with, he would now owe $176 more than he had received. He has paid $2,876 in interest and is indebted for more than he borrowed.

As you see, the amount of amortization is important, and a favorable rate should be negotiated when the mortgage is placed.

Not all second mortgages are so unfavorable as the one just mentioned.

• PURCHASE MONEY (P.M.) MORTGAGES

When banks are unwilling to provide sufficient financing or interest rates are so steep as to preclude the sale of property, it is not uncommon for an owner to give (take back) a mortgage himself if he is anxious to sell. In other words, instead of receiving the entire amount of the purchase price in cash, he takes part of it in monthly payments with interest. This mortgage is called a *purchase money (P.M.) mortgage*—so called because the loan was given in order to make the sale possible. Sometimes providing a mortgage, which makes the transaction an installment sale, is advantageous to the seller for income tax purposes.

A P.M. mortgage can be a first, second, or third mortgage, depending on the existing mortgaging at the time of sale. If the seller owns the house free and clear, the P.M. would be a first mortgage. If there is already mortgaging on the property, the P.M. would take its proper place behind existing mortgages. In some neighborhoods it is not uncommon for a property to have several mortgages— each a P.M. held by a previous owner.

Unlike previously mentioned second mortgages, a P.M. mortgage given by the seller is not discounted—the premium the seller receives is the sale of his property at a price agreeable to him. If he had to depend on a bank to give his buyer a new first mortgage, he might not be able to sell his house at all. If an owner is anxious to sell his property, he may even provide financing at a below-market interest rate.

- SUBORDINATION

If the seller gives you a P.M. mortgage and you plan to renovate, try also to get subordination. *Subordination* means that the mortgage does not have to be paid off first if a new first mortgage is placed on the property, but will instead revert to a secondary (or subordinate) position behind the new first mortgage.

To illustrate how subordination works, assume that a house has two mortgages, a first of $10,000 and a second of $5,000. If these are consolidated in a new first mortgage in the amount of $15,000, $10,000 of this money goes to pay off the existing first mortgage, and $5,000 goes to pay off the second mortgage. However, if the original second mortgage contained a subordination clause, it would not have to be paid off; it would revert to a secondary position behind the *new* first mortgage, and the owner would thus receive $5,000 in cash.

Subordination of a P.M. mortgage is the most favorable way to obtain the necessary money to purchase and renovate a house where adequate first mortgaging is not available. However, the seller most likely will want to place some restrictions on his subordination. For example, to protect his loan against overfinancing, the mortgagee will probably want to limit the size of the first mortgage that takes precedence over his P.M. so that he can reasonably expect to recoup his investment in case of default. He may also want to approve the first mortgagee. Subordination is a complex matter, and terms must be worked out in advance with the assistance of a knowledgeable attorney.

The value of a subordinated P.M. mortgage can be illustrated by the example of the John Does. They found a house that could be purchased for $30,000, and estimated that it would cost $20,000 to renovate—a total of $50,000. They had $5,000 in cash and no other convertible assets. Their bank was willing to provide a mortgage of only 75% of the value, or $37,500 on the finished house. That left the Does $7,500 away from the amount needed. Their seller then agreed to give them a $7,500 P.M. mortgage as part of the purchase agreement—and to subordinate that mortgage to their $37,500 bank mortgage. With a total of $45,000 in mortgaging, plus their $5,000 cash, the Does were able to buy and renovate the house.

- BALLOON MORTGAGE

An owner may agree to give a P.M. mortgage for only a short period, such as three to five years; thus if the mortgage is self-amortizing, the monthly payments will be extremely high. In such a situation, you might consider a *balloon mortgage*—a mortgage that is not self-amortizing, requiring a large principal payment (balloon) when the term expires. (The second mortgage discussed on page 140 was a balloon mortgage.) In such a loan the amortization can be very low or nonexistent. If you are paying interest only, you will have the entire principal to repay at the end of the mortgage term. Obviously a balloon mortgage is not wise unless you are fairly certain that the cash will be available to meet the debt, but in some circumstances it can make sense.

As renovation improves a run-down neighborhood, the neighborhood becomes more desirable and property values rise. Banks then become willing to give larger mortgages. Thus three to five years after you complete your renovation, your bank may give you a new mortgage large enough to cover both mortgages when your balloon mortgage comes due.

For example, in 1965, the John Smiths bought a rooming house for $25,000, which cost them an additional $25,000 to renovate to a three-family house. At the time, banks would lend no more than $25,000 regardless of how much was invested in the property. So the Smiths negotiated with the seller to give them a P.M. mortgage of $15,000, which he agreed to subordinate to the new

$25,000 first mortgage. The seller set a term of five years for his P.M. mortgage, but he agreed to the low amortization figure of 2% a year so that the Smiths could hold down their monthly costs. This meant that in five years the mortgage would be reduced by only $1,500, leaving a debt of $13,500 to be paid when the mortgage came due.

During that five years many houses in the area were renovated, and the purchase price for unrenovated houses more than doubled. With each year the Smiths' property became more valuable; banks were placing mortgages in excess of $50,000 on renovated property. The Smiths were able to refinance the entire cost of their house, recouping not only the amortization payments they had made, but their initial cash investment as well. You cannot necessarily assume that this will happen, but the situation is certainly not unique. In renvoation neighborhoods across the country property values have soared as the renovation movement snowballed.

However, there is one serious drawback to a balloon mortgage. What do you do if money is tight when your mortgage comes due and there is no money available for home mortgages? Or what do you do if interest rates are extremely high at the time you need to refinance, considerably escalating your mortgage payments? Both of these possibilities must be considered when taking on a balloon mortgage.

- THE VALUE OF REFINANCING

The property appreciation factor is a prime attraction to the real estate investor. Property appreciation enabled the John Smiths to refinance their house, consolidating two mortgages into one larger mortgage that had been unattainable five years before.

But refinancing also allows an owner to realize cash from his past amortization payments—plus an additional amount of money representing the appreciation value of the property. Of course, if you refinance for a larger amount, your mortgage payments will probably increase. But the mortgage can be replaced by a new one for the original amount (providing the interest rate and term remain the same) with no increase in monthly payments. The experienced real estate investor may often refinance every ten years in order to reinvest his cash elsewhere. Refinancing allows you to recoup your cash investment and realize appreciation without selling your house. What an easy way to pay for the children's college education, buy a summer house, or take a trip to Europe!

• FINANCING RENOVATION

You must first purchase the house and then pay for the renovation. Unless you have a substantial amount of cash, you will need to finance both. If you get a new mortgage in order to purchase, where do you get the money for renovation?

• The Construction Loan (Building Loan)

A *construction loan* is temporary financing designed to take you through construction to the finished product, on which a long-term permanent mortgage can be placed.

• *Points.* A construction loan involves a risk to the lender, because there is no guarantee that the job will be completed or that it will be done well. Because of the risk, construction financing is usually more expensive than permanent financing (first mortgages). Either the interest rate will be higher than the prevailing rate on mortgages or there will be a bonus charge called *points,* which is similar to the discount rate on second mortgages. The number of points means the percentage deducted from the amount of the loan: Two points would mean a 2% discount. Points are not limited to construction loans. When money is tight, points are often charged on first mortgages as well.

- ## COMBINATION MORTGAGES

The ideal type of financing for renovation is the *combination mortgage.* On this type of mortgage the lender agrees to give you a new first mortgage upon completion of construction, but meanwhile will give you a certain percentage (usually 90%) in the form of a construction loan. When the job is complete, the amount advanced for construction will be incorporated into a new first mortgage along with the final payment you will receive at the time the permanent mortgage is written. In the take-down schedule on 133, the first four payments would be for the construction loan, and the permanent mortgage would be written at the time of the fifth payment.

A more simplified form of the combination mortgage is used by many banks when the amount of money needed is not large. No construction loan is used, but the permanent mortgage is advanced in three or four stages, the first advance at the time of purchase and the final advance on completion of the renovation. Most often these mortgages have amortization payments during construction; and sometimes the full mortgage is recorded at the time of the first advance, with payments based on the full amount even though the balance of the mortgage is held in escrow by the lender until the next payment is released. This type of mortgage is tailor-made for the particular situation, so there is no standard procedure.

Some banks will not give construction money because of the risk. However, if a permanent mortgage commitment has been obtained from a bank, the owner can often get a construction loan from firms that specialize in construction financing. A construction loan, whether it is a separate loan or part of a combination mortgage, has a time limit, and the job must be completed within the specified time. The commitment for a permanent mortgage usually has a time limit also, after which the lender is not obligated to honor his commitment to provide the mortgage. Some renovators who were not aware of the importance of this time limit have found themselves in difficulty when construction work was not completed by the deadline. In some cases mortgagees are willing to extend the mortgage commitment, but raise the interest rate on the mortgage or charge an additional fee for the extension. Furthermore, you must remember that permanent mortgage commitments are based on the renovation you describe to the lender. If you make changes as the renovation progresses, the lender is not obligated to honor his commitment. So any major changes, particularly omissions of work previously planned, should be approved by the lender.

• HOME IMPROVEMENT LOANS

Another kind of financing available to help pay for renovation is the *home improvement loan.* It is a short-term loan, usually no more than three to five years, and it is discounted. It is relatively easy to obtain from most banks, but the amount that can be borrowed on a home improvement loan is limited. Because the term is short, the monthly payments are higher than those on mortgages. However, when an additional $5,000 is needed to finish a renovation, a home improvement loan can provide the solution.

• ADDITIONAL MORTGAGE INFORMATION

• *Escrow for Taxes and Insurance.* Mortgagees are concerned that their loan be secure, that the property be adequately insured against fire, and that real estate taxes are paid—since an uninsured fire can wipe out the lender's investment, and unpaid taxes can bring foreclosure proceedings by the city. Many lenders require monthly mortgage payments to include a pro-rated amount for taxes and insurance, with this money held in a special *(escrow)* account from which the lender makes payments as they are due. Mortgagees realize that it is often difficult for an owner to set aside money each month for bills that must be paid only once or twice a year. When the mortgage is placed, the cost of real estate taxes and insurance is determined and then divided by twelve to determine the monthly amount that must be added to the regular mortgage payment. If taxes or insurance premiums rise, the escrow payment is increased to cover the additional costs. Escrow payments for taxes and insurance are not always a condition of a first mortgage. When the borrower pays these bills himself, the lender normally requires proof that they have been paid.

• *Grace Period.* Each mortgage specifies the date on which payments are due, but there is a period of grace, usually specified in the mortgage, during which no foreclosure action can be taken because payment did not arrive on the date it was due. The borrower may incur a late charge if the payment is more than 10 to 15 days overdue. However, once the grace period has passed, the mortgagor is in default and the mortgagee can institute legal action for payment (foreclosure).

• A MORTGAGE CAN BE AN ASSET

Some people have the mistaken notion that a mortgage is something bad, to be gotten rid of as quickly as possible. No doubt this notion comes from the melodrama in which the villain (twirling his big black mustache) threatens to foreclose the mortgage and drive the heroine out into the snowstorm. This feeling about mortgages is also expressed in the custom of the mortgage button, found in old New England houses: when the mortgage was paid off, it was burned and the ashes placed inside the newel post in the front entrance hall. The small wooden "button" in the center of the top was replaced with an ivory button so that guests would know that the owner had paid off the mortgage.

However, if your mortgage is self-amortizing and at a favorable interest rate, you have nothing to gain and possibly a great deal to lose by paying it off ahead of time simply to remove the debt. If you would like to lower your operating costs, you can do so in ways other than paying off the mortgage. The money you would use to remove the mortgage can be invested, and you can use the return on that investment to make your mortgage payments. You would then have two investments instead of one, both of which could appreciate in value. And your favorable mortgage could be an asset if you wanted to sell the house.

Although mortgages as such are not bad, there is such a thing as being overmortgaged. There has been a lot written about owning real estate with little or no cash investment, which is fine as long as the owner can afford to make the payments on all the money he has borrowed. If not, he is definitely overmortgaged!

• GOVERNMENT FINANCING PROGRAMS AND PURCHASE IN PROJECT AREAS

In addition to conventional financing, there are government mortgage programs (federal, state, and city) that provide money for building and/or renovation of housing, for which conventional lenders are unwilling or unable to give mortgages.

• FHA MORTGAGE INSURANCE PROGRAMS

Under these programs, the federal government itself does not give mortgages. It insures, or guarantees, mortgages made by approved lenders—banks, building and loan associations, and so on. There are many different FHA mortgage insurance programs, each with its own qualifications designed to carry out the various objectives of the federal government. The FHA and its first programs were created to encourage and make home ownership possible for large numbers of American families who had good credit but insufficient capital to purchase homes.

Prior to the establishment of FHA in 1934, most mortgages were short-term balloon mortgages with average terms of three years and no set amortization of payments. Usually all an owner could do was keep up with interest payments and periodically renew the loan. Therefore, people saved for years, often well into middle age, to pay cash for their homes so there could be no danger of foreclosure.

FHA-insured mortgages were self-amortizing and extended the debt over a long period of time. This FHA policy helped make the low down payment, fully amortized loan the standard mortgaging practice of lending institutions.

Under the FHA mortgage and loan insurance system, a buyer makes a small down payment and obtains a mortgage for the rest of the purchase price. The mortgage loan is made by an FHA-approved lender and insured by FHA, which means that the lender has a guarantee that his loan will be made good. Because he has no risks, the lender can allow more liberal terms than would otherwise be possible.

FHA-insured mortgages often offer more liberal conditions than their conventional counterparts, and can cover up to 100% of appraised value in some instances.

FHA charges a mortgage insurance premium of ½% a year on the average outstanding balance. This premium is in addition to the interest and amortization payments, but is included in the monthly mortgage payment and is disbursed to FHA by the lender. Considering the liberal terms, the premium charged by FHA is worth paying.

FHA mortgage insurance programs cover financing for new and used houses, for new construction and renovation, for purchase and refinancing, for private homes and multiple dwellings, for property in urban, suburban, and rural areas. There is hardly a category of residential housing not covered by some FHA program.

Each FHA program has a set of minimum property standards that must be met, and a ratio of loan-to-value (or cost) used to determine the amount of the mortgage to be insured. Each program has a maximum loan amount and a maximum mortgage term: The amount and term of a mortgage are determined by FHA when an application is received.

In order to qualify for FHA insurance, the borrower must have a good credit record and enough steady income to meet mortgage payments and other operating expenses of the property without difficulty. In addition, the property must meet the requirements set by FHA for the particular program involved. Information on all FHA programs can be obtained from the following:

1. U.S. Department of Housing and Urban Development (HUD), Washington, D.C.
2. Regional HUD office for your area (address can be obtained from HUD in Washington or from FHA)
3. Federal Housing Administration, Washington, D.C.
4. Local FHA office in your city (check phone book for address and number)

The Veterans Administration (VA) has loan programs for qualified veterans. There are also state and city loan programs available for specialized situations. Some of these involve the upgrading of rundown property and neighborhoods. Contact appropriate government offices to see if there are programs that might be helpful to you.

Columns play an important part in Southern architecture. These restored Atlanta houses are typical of early twentieth-century architecture in most Southern cities and towns.

9 | Purchasing a House

DUE TO a lack of knowledge, the inexperienced buyer usually does very little negotiating when purchasing a house. The price of the house and the amount of cash needed are the major concerns, and even these may be accepted by a naive purchaser without negotiation. But the purchase of a house can be complex, particularly when mortgage money is difficult to obtain, when interest rates are high, and/or the buyer plans extensive renovation. Under these circumstances the terms of the purchase can be as important as the price. When buying a house to renovate, one must consider financing, building codes, zoning restrictions, and many other factors.

There are three steps involved in buying a house: negotiating the purchase; signing the purchase contract (going to contract); and taking title to the property (closing).

Once the buyer and seller have agreed on the price and terms of purchase, a contract that details this agreement is drawn up and signed by both parties. Even though a verbal agreement has been reached, either side can back out with very little liability prior to signing a contract. If, however, a broker is involved in the transactions, he can sue for his commission once a verbal agreement has been reached, because he has fulfilled his responsibility to find a buyer who is ready, willing, and able to purchase. Many real estate brokers do not involve themselves in verbal negotiations: offers are frequently made by brokers on standard contracts. When such an offer is signed by both buyer and seller, it becomes a legally binding contract, and if the buyer reneges, he usually forfeits his deposit. He can also be sued to enforce the sale. Therefore, do not sign a sale contract unless you are sure you want to buy the property.

Once all the conditions of the sale contract have been met, a closing takes place, in which the title to the property changes hands. The closing is a mere formality. The signing of the contract is the critical phase in purchasing.

· HIRING A LAWYER

An attorney is needed in all real estate transactions. He handles the closing, seeing that all terms of the contract have been met. If the sale involves new financing, the lender will have an attorney do the necessary legal work and you will pay his fee. Most lending institutions have their own attorneys who handle all their legal work; but sometimes you can negotiate with the lender to allow you to use your own attorney to handle the closing. No matter how simple the transaction, an attorney is needed to consummate the sale of real estate.

Since buying a house for renovation is seldom a simple transaction, it is wise to consult a knowledgeable real estate lawyer before you even begin to look at property and certainly before you begin serious negotiations for purchase. You not only want the smartest lawyer you can find, but one who will take an interest in your affairs and is thoroughly familiar with the kinds of problems you will face.

You are not drawing up a will, so for heaven's sake do not depend on Aunt Jane's lawyer, ever so nice though he may be. You are buying a city house, which often encompasses a multitude of sins and building violations. You need an astute real estate attorney who is familiar with the type of property you are buying and the renovation you will undertake. You need someone to represent you who will insure that you get everything you bargained for and nothing more. Talk to several lawyers, if necessary, until you find one in whom you have confidence.

Make an appointment to go to the lawyer's office before you begin negotiations to purchase. Tell him what you have in mind, and ask for his suggestions. Discuss with him the services he can provide and the fee he will charge.

Do not pinch pennies with your lawyer. He will work diligently for you and your interests only if you are willing to compensate him for his efforts. The experience of the lawyer can often save you the cost of his fee, and perhaps more, by avoiding potential problems. However, legal fees can mount quickly. The ideal solution is to negotiate in advance a fixed fee for the various services you will need. If this is not possible because of the complexities of your situation, get a set hourly rate and ask for an agreed-upon maximum fee. If the lawyer you decide to use will only work on an hourly basis, insist upon a regular accounting of the amount you owe so that you are not hit by a staggering legal bill at the end of your project. If you plan to use a lawyer for more than the closing, paying him in installments is much easier than handling a large bill when all his work is complete. (Should you feel your lawyer's bill is excessive, discuss it with him. Although they do not publicize it, lawyer's fees are sometimes negotiable.)

You may need your lawyer's advice throughout the entire project. In addition to handling the legal work for purchase and financing, he can be consulted on contracts for renovation, and he can advise you on tax problems concerning the property, the kind of insurance you should carry, and the form of ownership the house should be in.

Ownership of property can be individual (one person), multiple (two or more people), or corporate (a corporation having title to the property with individuals owning shares in the corporation) or otherwise. Each type of ownership has advantages and disadvantages. In individual and multiple ownership, the owner(s) is personally responsible for the expenses and operation of the property; in corporate ownership the corporation (rather than the officers or shareholders) is responsible for the property. In individual or multiple ownership, all expenses can be deducted from the personal income of the owner(s); in corporate ownership, the corporation, not the shareholders, receives any tax benefits of ownership. (See Appendix for discussion of tax benefits.)

Sometimes, particularly during construction, it may be advantageous to have the property in a wife's name or in a corporation to protect other assets such as salary or investments. Although property ownership can be transferred, there are legal and tax considerations in such transactions as well as in the decision about the form of ownership. These should be discussed with a lawyer and/or accountant.

An attorney's job is to be your legal representative. He should point out potential problems, but it is not his job to make decisions for you. His knowledge of city regulations, codes, zoning, restrictive covenants, and mortgaging can prevent unforeseen disasters.

His job is to see that you are protected legally in every way possible. If he is to represent you properly, he must have all the facts. He must see that the contract for purchase contains everything that the seller has agreed to, that it has no hidden provisions of which the buyer is unaware, and that the purchaser will be given a clear title to the property.

• NEGOTIATING THE PURCHASE

In negotiating a purchase, you should attempt to buy under the most favorable conditions. The price to be paid for the house is only one of the terms of purchase. Other terms that may be important are:

1. The amount of cash needed to purchase
2. The financing available (either existing mortgages or P.M. mortgage provided by the seller)*
3. Whether the sale is conditioned on the buyer's ability to get new financing (conditional sale)
4. Whether the house is purchased occupied or vacant
5. Whether the property is sold in as-is condition
6. The contents of the house that are to be a part of the sale
7. The amount of down payment, and how this money will be handled
8. The closing date, and interim access to the property for the buyer

The buyer should determine in advance the key items that must be negotiated. Negotiations are usually a matter of compromise, with neither party getting everything he asks for. The buyer should know which items are non-negotiable. If the key item is financing by the seller, the buyer may have to pay the asking price or even a little more, whereas if the sale is for all cash (or cash over existing mortgages) the buyer can expect to bargain on the price. At the beginning, the buyer should clearly state to the broker or owner those terms that are absolutely necessary for purchase. If no agreement can be reached on these, there is no sense wasting time on other points.

*See Chapter 8.

- THE CASH NEEDED TO PURCHASE

The amount of cash may or may not be critical to the seller, but it definitely is important to the buyer. When renovation is planned, the buyer cannot afford to put all of his cash into the purchase. He must have enough money to pay lawyer, architect, and other miscellaneous costs involved in starting the renovation. Generally speaking, the less cash paid, the better for the buyer. It is always a good idea to have more cash available than you think you will need in case unforeseen difficulties arise during construction. You may need more cash during periods of construction than you will have invested in the house when it is completed: money may be owed before the bank releases it to you for payment. Keep this in mind when negotiating the cash required for purchase.

The cash payment for the house can be lowered by the use of financing. If the price of the property is $30,000, the amount of cash needed will depend on the financing. If there is an existing $15,000 mortgage, the buyer must pay $15,000 in cash for the house unless the seller is willing to take back a mortgage or the buyer can obtain a new mortgage for a larger amount. If the seller is willing to hold an additional $10,000 mortgage, the buyer will need only $5,000 in cash to purchase.

If the owner is inflexible in the amount of cash he requires, and that amount falls within your budget, get him to negotiate on other points.

- EXISTING MORTGAGES, P.M. MORTGAGE, AND SUBORDINATION

The property you are planning to buy may or may not have existing mortgages. If it does, you should be given information about them. (See pages 112–13 for the information you will need.) If there is no due-on-sale clause, the current mortgages on the property will remain when you take title unless you or the seller chooses to pay them off. Thus, if a house selling for $20,000 had $7,000 in mortgaging, you would pay the seller $13,000 in cash and take over the $7,000 worth of mortgaging. If the mortgage has no provision for prepayment, you will not be able to refinance the property until the mortgage expires, unless you pay penalties. (If there is a prepayment penalty, you may want to negotiate with the seller to compensate you for the amount of the penalty.) If the payments on existing mortgages are extremely high, you may want to get a new mortgage for a longer term to lower payments. If the interest rate on the existing mortgage is below the current rate, you may want to keep them on the property as long as possible. You will be unable to make a judgment about existing mortgages until you have all the facts about them.

Often the asking price of the property is more than the combination of asking cash and existing mortgages. In such cases, the seller may plan to take back a P.M. mortgage. (See page 141). All the terms of the P.M. must be negotiated—amount, interest rate, term, and so forth. Be sure that you understand what you need when negotiating the P.M.

It is a good idea to try to get subordination of this mortgage (see page 142), even if you do not think you will need it. You do not have to use the subordination clause, but it is generally impossible to obtain subordination once the mortgage has been written.

Subordination is a very complex matter and should be discussed in detail with a lawyer before any agreement has been reached. The subordination agreement must be meaningful and legally enforcible. Only a lawyer can assist you in negotiating proper subordination for a mortgage.

• CONDITIONAL SALE

If the seller is unwilling to take back a mortgage when the amount of cash asked is more than you have, you must get a new mortgage in order to purchase the house. In such a situation, you should insist on a *conditional sale.* This means that the sale is conditioned on your ability to get a mortgage of a specified amount. The sale price and all other terms of purchase are agreed upon and incorporated into a sale contract that is binding on you only if you are able to get the necessary financing. However, all the terms of the mortgage you seek must be spelled out in the contract so that you are not forced to accept unfavorable terms. Your down payment is refunded if no such mortgage can be obtained. If you do not have a conditional contract and are unable to get a mortgage, you will lose your down payment deposit and may be liable for damages.

A conditional sale is binding on the seller: his property is taken off the market while you look for a mortgage. You have a specified amount of time to get the mortgage, which must be negotiated in the conditional sale terms.

• THE PROBLEM OF VACATING

Vacating a house may be a problem, depending on whether the tenants have leases, the type of tenants involved, and local regulations dealing with vacating. For the inexperienced, the process is neither easy nor pleasant. In some areas vacating is very difficult, or even impossible because of rent control regulations.*

---

*If you plan to buy a house in New York, for instance, rent control or rent stabilization can present serious problems. Not only does it affect your ability to get possession of your house, but it can also affect the amount of rent you can charge tenants, as well as future rent increases. Be *sure* that you discuss these problems with a knowledgeable lawyer before buying a house in any location that has such laws.

The seller is in a much better position to vacate than you are because he knows the tenants. Try to get him to sell you a vacant house. That way, you know that you can start renovation whenever you are ready and will not have to wait for tenants to move or supply them with services while they remain. It is often worthwhile to pay more for the house to have it delivered vacant. Discuss the problem of vacating with your lawyer before deciding to undertake the job yourself.

If you should decide to buy an occupied property, remember that there may be additional expenses for vacating that will add to the cost of the finished house. Many cities have regulations requiring the owner to pay relocation fees to displaced tenants. You may have to find new homes for tenants in order to speed the vacating process. In some cities there are firms or individuals that can be hired to vacate property. (An owner's time is generally better spent in planning the renovation than in relocating tenants.)

Ask your lawyer or real estate broker for the names of people who can be hired to vacate your property for you.

• THE CONDITION OF THE PROPERTY WHEN PURCHASED

Most property is sold as is, with no guarantees given on its condition. Sometimes a seller is willing to give guarantees as to the condition of the property and occasionally you will find an owner willing to rectify certain conditions, such as a leaky roof, before you take title to the house. (You may want to do this work yourself to see that it is properly done. If so, ask for a price reduction instead.) Any conditions in the property that are to be changed by the owner must be negotiated and incorporated in the sale contract.

Old city houses often have building violations, some of which may be on record with the building department as uncorrected. If you are planning to do a major renovation, they may not be important, since construction will usually remove them. However, your lawyer may insist upon having a record of any violations on file so that you are aware of the problems you face. This information is often a good bargaining point when dealing with the owner of a house in bad condition.

• THE CONTENTS OF THE HOUSE

The sale of a house usually includes built-in features of the property. However, the lovely dining-room chandelier that enticed you to buy the house may be missing the day you take title unless you negotiate for it to remain and include this agreement in the sale contract. On the other hand, the house may be full of furniture and debris. If you expect the seller to remove it, you must negotiate for this also. In some localities refrigerators are not considered built-in features and may not remain when a house is sold, nor are they included by landlords in rental units.

• DOWN PAYMENT ON CONTRACT

The amount of down payment is often a matter of local practice. It can be a flat amount, regardless of the price of the property, or it can be a percentage of either the sale price or the amount of cash to be paid at closing. The seller usually wants a large deposit to discourage default on the contract, while the buyer prefers to tie up as little cash as possible. However, if you are making a low offer on a house you really want, a larger than normal down payment is often a useful tool in negotiating.

What happens to this down payment is important to you. If the money is given directly to the seller, you may have difficulty recouping it if the sale falls through and you are entitled to a refund. To avoid any such problem, you should insist that the money be held in escrow by a third party (either the real estate broker or the seller's attorney) until title to the property changes hands. If the seller reneges on the contract or is unable to deliver clear title, the money is returned to you. If you back out of the agreement, the money may be turned over to the seller. However, you can specify in the contract that any earnest money be returned to you if the sale is not consummated for any reason.

- DATE FOR TAKING TITLE

Most sale contracts call for title to change hands as soon as all the conditions of the contract can be met. This usually takes no longer than thirty days. Often, however, a buyer would like to have a longer period of time between contract and closing. Since a seller can terminate a contract if too many delays are requested, you should negotiate in advance for enough time. A sixty- or ninety-day contract is not unusual.

- RIGHT OF ACCESS

You should insure your rights to visit the property during the contract period in order to start planning the renovation. Negotiate this right as a part of the sale agreement. It is not unusual to start drawing the plans for renovation before you have title to the property. In fact, you can save time and carrying costs by arranging to have the renovation planning done during the contract period so you are ready to start work once you take title to the house. There is always the chance that the sale will not go through, causing you to lose any money spent on plans. Whether to take this risk is up to you. However, under no circumstances should you perform any physical work on the property until you take title. It is extremely risky to invest money in a house you do not own. If the sale were not consummated, you would not only lose any money invested, but would be liable for damages as well.

• THE SALE CONTRACT

The sale contract is the legal document on which the sale of property is based. It contains the sale price and all terms and conditions of sale. Any agreement between you and the seller must be incorporated in the contract to be legally binding. (Verbal agreements normally cannot be enforced.)

Many houses are sold through real estate brokers who present buyer's offers to sellers on standard sales contracts. Once one of these contracts is signed by buyer and seller, it is a legally binding document. If you make an offer to purchase in writing and it is witnessed, you may have bought yourself a piece of property, so be sure you understand all of the fine print. If you plan to buy through a real estate broker, get a copy of his sales contract in advance and go over it with your lawyer.

A sale contract is written in legal jargon that is not only boring to read, but difficult to understand. It is your lawyer's job to see that the contract contains all provisions agreed upon, that these provisions can be enforced, that you will receive a clear title to the property, and that you are not being cheated. When there is no real estate broker involved, or where the broker doesn't use his own sales contract, the contract is normally drawn up by the seller's attorney and is approved or amended as necessary by your attorney. The ideal procedure is to have the contract drawn up in advance so that the lawyers can iron out the difficulties before signing day. When this is done, you are often unaware of the work the lawyer had done in your behalf.

When the contract is not drawn up in advance, your attorney has his first opportunity to see the document the day it is to be signed, and the session can be a long and noisy one. The contract will often look more like a doodle sheet than a legal document, with all changes and additions handwritten and initialed by both you and the seller.

Once the contract is complete and approved by both attorneys, you and the seller sign it and you make a down payment.

• BETWEEN CONTRACT AND CLOSING

During this interval your lawyer, or the lawyer for the bank if an institutional mortgage is involved, will be preparing for the closing. The title to the property must be searched and title insurance obtained. A *title search* is an examination of public records to determine the ownership, encumbrances, encroachments, and rights of way affecting real property. (Ask your lawyer if a mineral search should be made as well, because mineral rights and surface rights may be separate.) *Title insurance* is an insurance policy that indemnifies the holder for any loss sustained by reason of defects in the title. Although there is little prospect of difficulty once the title has been searched, there is no reason to take a chance when title insurance is available at such reasonable cost. If an institutional mortgage is involved, the lender will insist on title insurance to cover the amount of his loan, in which case the lender will be named the beneficiary. Although you pay the premium, you will have no coverage. Ask the lawyer about the advisability of getting a Title Insurance Policy for yourself.

Your lawyer will have a *survey** of the property made (or the existing one updated), verify existing mortgages, and check the property for liens and violations. Your lawyer will make sure that the title is free of defects and that you are protected in every way possible.

Meanwile, there are matters that you should take care of. You should notify electric and gas companies to have the utilities transferred to your name on the date of clos-

---

*A survey is not always a part of the sale. It is an additional expense if not required, but it is recommended. It is always best to know exactly where property lines are located and to be sure there are no problems.

ing. If heat is provided by oil, you should make arrangement for fuel-oil deliveries and service of the furance. You must also be certain that the property will be adequately covered by insurance when you take title. (See Appendix, page 000, for information on insurance.)

· THE CLOSING

When all the terms and conditions of the contract have been met, the closing takes place. It is here that the property changes hands. You give the seller a certified check for the amount you owe, and he gives you the deed to the property. The change in ownership is recorded and becomes a matter of public record.

At the closing, there are *adjustments* to be made on real estate taxes, mortgage payments, insurance, water and sewer charges, and fuel and utility bills. If any of these items has been paid in advance by the seller, he will receive a refund for the portion that does not apply to his ownership. If, however, bills are owing for debts incurred during the seller's ownership, you will receive credit.

In addition to adjustments, there will be *closing costs* for the purchase. These consist of title insurance, survey cost, tax stamps, recording fees, and other miscellaneous charges. These costs are normally paid by the purchaser, and your lawyer should give you an estimate of the amount in advance of the closing date.

The closing can be handled exclusively by the attorneys without the buyer or seller being present. However, most buyers want to be present at this official ceremony. When the closing is complete, the buyer has become the proud (and often poor) owner of a piece of real estate. It is not uncommon for buyer and lawyer to have a drink to celebrate the transaction.

· KEEPING RECORDS

Now that you own a house, it is very important to keep accurate records of all money spent on it. Ideally all expenditures should be made by check, with a notation at the bottom relating it to the house. (At income tax time you may have forgotten who John Doe is, from whom you bought that old mantel to replace the missing one.) If payments are made in cash, be sure to get a receipt and file it with other house records. Many people who insist on receiving cash can be paid by making out the check in their name, having them endorse it, and cashing it for them. Many contractors use this method of paying workmen so they have proof of payment in the canceled check.

It is amazing how many boxes of nails and miscellaneous items you can buy, and these trivial expenses can add up. You want to be able to get every tax advantage possible, and this can be done only if accurate records have been kept.

It is also important to know exactly how much you have invested in your house if you should sell it. Any improvements after the renovation is finished should be recorded, even though there is no tax deduction on your own living quarters: the expenditures *will* make a difference if you sell the property, for they may enable you to avoid a capital-gains tax at the time of sale.

If the property brings in rental income, it is mandatory that you keep a record book of income and expenses. At tax time you will have all the necessary information already recorded, making preparation of income tax returns much easier.

It is always best to discuss record keeping with either your lawyer or accountant, who can acquaint you with procedures and tell you what records must be kept.

These two houses, both located in Atlanta's Inman Park Historic District, were renovated by Martha Stamm Connell. Both were covered with asbestos siding and required extensive renovation inside and out, including new plumbing, wiring, heating and air conditioning systems, and new roofs. Each house was small, but because of the extremely high-pitched roofs, unused attic space was utilized by installing spiral stairs to a new master bedroom and bath.

| 10 | The Basic Elements of a Renovation |

• THE IMPORTANCE OF PLANNING

Having a total plan for your house before you begin is vitally important. *Do not tear out one wall or drive one nail before you have a plan for the finished house.* This is as important for a simple renovation as for a major one, and is perhaps more necessary for piecemeal, long-term remodeling than for a job to be completed in a matter of months, where a plan is more likely to be an integral part of the project.

Most renovators are so anxious to see work begin that they plunge in headlong without proper preparation. Some people have managed to muddle through on luck, but others find themselves with expensive kitchens or bathrooms immovably installed in places where they are not wanted.

A young couple bought a house in Brooklyn that had been renovated into several small apartments. They moved into the ground floor, planning to take over the parlor floor when their budget allowed them to create a two-story apartment for themselves. The kitchen was miserably inadequate, so as soon as they were able to scrape together enough money, they remodeled it with new appliances and cabinets. When they took over the parlor floor, they discovered that the kitchen was in the wrong place and did not function within the framework of the newly added space, but they had invested too much money to contemplate ripping it out and starting over, since the cabinets and appliances could not be sensibly reused. Had they only formulated a plan for the finished apartment before they remodeled the kitchen, they could have worked out a solution that would have functioned well before and after. As you can see, the less money you have, the more important it is to have a total plan.

The most serious and costly problems that occur in construction are usually the result of inadequate planning and could be avoided by taking the time to think out every detail carefully in advance. The first step involves an assessment of the current condition of the house, both interior and exterior. An evaluation must be made of the existing plumbing and wiring, the roof, gutters and leaders, and exterior, including foundations. (If you followed advice urging professional inspection before purchase, you should already have a written report on these conditions. If you did not, have it done *now*.) Deficiencies in any of the above should be corrected before any other work is begun. While it is an entirely normal impulse to want to rush in and do things that show, such as painting and wallpapering or a new kitchen, it could be a heartbreaking mistake. If a room is decorated before the old plumbing is replaced, there is a danger of water damage as well as the possibility that walls must be ripped open for repairs. If the roof should leak, a ceiling may fall, or at the very least, plaster will crack and discolor. If the exterior walls have any cracks or gaps, there is a constant danger of water damage and the added expense of heat loss. Work done on a floor-at-a-time basis can result in an enormous waste of money, as completed work on lower floors may be damaged by construction above. This is not to say that you cannot renovate your house gradually; only plan carefully in advance so that work is done in the proper sequence. Lack of planning may end well through sheer luck, as it did for a couple who bought an eighteenth-century house in Old Town, Alexandria, Virginia. Buying on impulse and having to sell everything conceivable to raise the cash they needed, they did nothing about having the house inspected by a professional, and felt they could not afford an architect or contractor. They were under the illusion that they could simply clean up and paint to make their house habitable. Like so many of us, they never considered those vital unseen elements whose functions we take for granted, such as plumbing, wiring, and heating. They had never even heard of a bearing wall.*

Since the kitchen was the worst room in the house, they decided to work on it first. They had their hearts set on a brick floor in their kitchen: when they ripped up the old flooring, they found they were standing on dirt. Further investigation revealed that there was nothing under the dining- or living-room floors either—the beams had been eaten away by dry rot, and all that propped up the floor were a few rocks under the center.

By this time they were aware that they needed new wiring, plumbing, and heating to replace the pipes that ran crazily around the walls. However, it was the bricklayer who advised them that the pipes and wiring must be installed first underneath before he laid the brick floor in the kitchen.

The living-room mantel was a later addition that did not conform to the period, so they ripped it off, only to discover bricks falling out of the wall and beaverboard

*A wall that is a structural component of the house and carries part of the load (weight) of the floors above.

propped in the gaps. Before they knew it, they had demolished the living room. The bricklayer reported that the chimney was a disaster, with scorched boards all around it. It had to be rebuilt from the top to bottom.

Fortunately, Alexandria is a tightly knit community with some excellent (and honest) craftsmen, so the couple survived and achieved a charming, beautifully restored house. However, they could have avoided their problems by having the house inspected before purchase. If they had bought it in spite of its defects, they would have known what to expect and been able to plan accordingly.

Begin to plan by looking carefully at the place you are currently living in. What do you like about it? What do you dislike? Look at your friends' homes, and evaluate how they would work for you. Make a list of what you would like to have in a house and what you would like to avoid. At all times you must keep finances in mind.

Before getting your plans on paper, you must understand the elements of a renovation and how they relate to one another. There are five general areas:

1. *Mechanical systems* (plumbing, wiring, heating, air conditioning, and mechanical ventilation): all of these systems are important because they provide essential services and conveniences. You may be able to use those currently existing in your house, but some, even if they are in good condition, may be inadequate for your needs and will have to be replaced or expanded. You should have an idea from the professional inspection what can be salvaged and what cannot.
2. *Room arrangement* (the floor plan)
3. *Equipment* (fixtures, cabinets, and appliances)
4. *Decorating* (flooring, painting, etc.)
5. *Landscaping*

You are probably familiar with the last four: the first seems a dreadful bore and is often swept under the carpet, either because the renovator is unaware of its importance or because he is too preoccupied with the kind of stove he will buy to think about whether there is a gas line that will make it work. While it is natural to be excited about the things that make a house attractive and pleasant, first things must come first, both in planning and construction. The mechanical systems must be considered first because they provide the necessary comforts that few of us are willing to do without—and you cannot decide where to put the dishwasher until you know where the plumbing and wiring will be. The dishwasher would be singularly useless without either.

· PLUMBING

Plumbing is a convenience that none of us would consider giving up. In addition to basic bath and kitchen facilities, it enables us to have such labor-saving devices as washing machines, dishwashers, and garbage disposals. Yet no other single item in a house can cause more annoyance, damage, and expense when it fails to function properly. Plumbing is an essential element of any renovation effort, and yet it is probably the least understood. If you are to plan and execute a renovation and hold your cost down, understanding the fundamentals of plumbing is essential. This knowledge will also enable you to see that your plumbing is installed properly when construction begins.

The plumbing system in any house consists of water pipes, which carry hot and cold water; soil (or waste) pipes, which carry water and waste to the sewer; and gas pipes. Most cities provide a public water supply and a public sewer system, each of which is usually located below ground in front of the property. (The local utility company's gas supply lines normally run in the same location.) The city also has a plumbing code, which is part of the Building Code: rules and regulations about plumbing— the kinds and sizes of pipes that can be used and how they must be installed and maintained. The code usually requires that new plumbing pipes be installed by licensed plumbers. Although plumbing codes vary from city to city, there are certain fundamentals of plumbing that apply everywhere.

• WATER LINES

There is a water line below ground that brings water from the city water supply (main) to the house; the installation and maintenance of this line is the responsibility of the property owner. Once inside the house, this supply line must be divided into two separate lines—one for cold water and one for hot. Hot water is obtained by feeding cold water into a *hot water heater* or into a *heating coil* that is part of the furnace. However the water is heated, you want to make sure that there is an adequate supply of hot water at all times by having a heater or coil large enough for the demands made on it. Water heaters can either be heated by the furnace or separately heated so that the furnace does not have to be on in hot weather.

A pair of water lines called *risers* are then run vertically through the house with pipes called *branches* connecting plumbing fixtures to the risers. The size of pipe needed for water lines will be determined by the number of fixtures and appliances serviced by the risers and by how high the risers must run. Risers are normally larger than branches, because constant pressure must be maintained in the risers even when one of the branch lines is turned on. If risers are too small, you will get a dribble when you should have strong pressure. Inadequate water pressure is a common problem in old houses. Many times the original water lines, which were installed to service only one bath, have been employed to serve several baths and/or kitchens, resulting in loss of water pressure at the top of the house when water is turned on below. This is usually the sign that water lines are too small for the use to which they are put.

When indoor plumbing came into use, water lines were made of lead (many old houses still contain some or all of the original lead pipes). Since then, water pipes have gone through an evolution of iron, steel, brass, and copper, with the latest innovation the introduction of plastic pipe. Although plastic piping has been endorsed as efficient and economical in certain situations by engineers and other professionals, many building codes do not allow its use— brass or copper is generally required for new water lines.

It is possible to continue using existing water lines when they are in the right location, are large enough, and are in good condition. However, you will often find that the water lines in old houses are a combination of various kinds of pipe, copper or brass mixed with lead or galvanized pipe. This combination of metals causes corrosion at the joints, resulting in leaks and broken pipes.

Do not take a chance on existing pipes that are in poor condition. A completely modernized and correctly installed plumbing system will give years of repair-free service. No one wants to go through the ordeal of major plumbing work once the renovation is completed. DON'T SCRIMP ON PLUMBING RENOVATION. Immediate savings will only increase the cost in the long run and cause headaches in the future.

• SOIL LINES

Each plumbing fixture must have a soil pipe, which takes water and waste to the sewer. It would obviously be very expensive to run a separate pipe from each fixture to the sewer; therefore, a vertical soil line, called a *stack*, is brought up through the house, and the fixtures in the house are attached to it by means of pipes called *branches.* Gases from the decomposition of waste are generated in the soil lines. To prevent these gases, odors, and actual waste from backing up into the fixtures, two things are done. First, each fixture has a *trap* connected to the drain pipe close to the fixture. This trap, an S-shaped pipe, holds a certain amount of water at all times through which gases cannot force their way. (The trap is the curved pipe you see under every sink.) In addition, the soil stack must be opened at the top so that sufficient fresh air can be supplied to the stack and branches through *vent pipes* to prevent back-up of waste material into fixtures and to dilute sewer gas. Every soil stack must go all the way through the roof. Each fixture must be connected to both the vent and the soil stack. The following illustration shows a soil stack, vent stack, and the branches of each.

Plumbing diagram

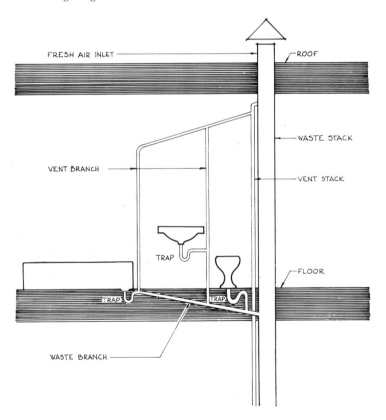

All of the pipes shown above would be hidden in the walls with the exception of the sink trap. Additional plumbing facilities could be installed on the other side of the stack and on the floor below by connecting these fixtures to the stack with additional branches. Notice that the above illustration shows the soil branch on a slant. If soil branches were horizontal, water and waste would not flow easily into the stack, but would tend to lie and accumulate in the pipe. All soil pipes that are not vertical must have a slope sufficient to insure immediate removal of waste to the sewer.

The soil stack is connected in the cellar to the *house drain.* The house drain is a large cast-iron pipe that normally runs (sloping) along a side wall, or along the floor, disappearing below ground at the front of the cellar. The house drain goes through the foundation wall and is joined to the *house sewer,* a large pipe connecting the house drain with the city sewer. (The installation and repair of the house sewer is the responsibility of the property owner.) The exterior gutters and leaders as well as the yard drains are connected to the house drain so that all water and waste is transported to the sewer.

Provisions must be made for cleaning out the drains and stacks in case of stoppage. This is done in the cellar by means of special plumbing fittings that have removable caps. These fittings are called *clean-outs,* and enough of them must be installed in the proper locations so that all lines can be properly cleaned out.

If soil lines are in good condition, are in the proper location for the baths and kitchens you need, and are large enough to service the fixtures and appliances you plan to install, there is no reason to replace them. Soil lines are generally cast iron, and the size required depends on the amount of waste they must dispose of. Be sure they are large enough to handle normal usage without clogging, and be sure that all lines are vented. Without proper venting you may find suds from the kitchen bubbling up in the bathroom sink, or possibly worse things.

• NEW PLUMBING INSTALLATION

If your plumbing is in the right location for the kitchens and baths you need and if it is in reusable condition, count yourself extremely fortunate indeed. (Do not forget to check the condition of the house sewer and water supply line from the street.) Being able to use existing plumbing can save a great deal of money.

If new plumbing is necessary, you must have more information before planning for it. Since the installation of new pipes is expensive, you should plan your room arrangement so that unnecessary plumbing costs are avoided. The location of baths, kitchens, and other plumbing facilities determines to some degree the price of the plumbing installation. One *line of plumbing* (soil stack, vent stack, and water risers) can serve many different plumbing facilities. The location of these facilities will determine whether more than one plumbing line is required. The examples shown on page 273 are an illustration:

Example A shows a situation where a separate plumbing line is needed for each bath because the distance between the two rooms is too great for both to be served by one line. The two plumbing lines are indicated by ○○○ inside the walls at either side of the plan. Example B shows how a simple modification of the plan will allow one line (located in the joint wall and indicated by ○○○) to serve both baths. From the point of construction, there is no difference between the two plans—each requires the same number of partitions. However, the difference in plumbing costs between the two is great.

Example B makes use of what is called *back-to-back plumbing*. When two rooms, both of which require plumbing, are placed back-to-back, one plumbing line located in the common wall can serve both areas. If the location of plumbing facilities is the same on two or more floors, the same line will serve each of these facilities. This is called *stacked plumbing*. In stacked plumbing, the plumbing facilities can be on either or both sides of the plumbing line. You can combine stacked and back-to-back plumbing to serve any number of needs. Thus it is possible to have all plumbing needs served by one plumbing line. This method of plumbing installation is the most economical and easiest.

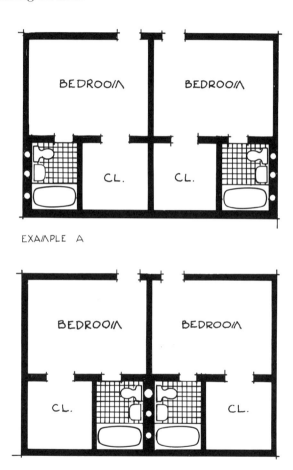

EXAMPLE A

EXAMPLE B

○   ○   ○ INDICATE PLUMBING LINES (OR STACKS)

Running the plumbing line vertically through the house is not always possible. Where the location of the plumbing line must change between floors, there may be problems. The soil stack must either be vertical or sloped sufficiently to allow waste to flow properly. If the shift in location occurs within a wall that can accommodate the necessary slope of the stack, there is no problem. However, if the shift in location of the stack involves crossing a room, there may not be sufficient space for the necessary slope of the stack. For this reason, baths and kitchens cannot be located on a mere whim—the problem of providing plumbing to these rooms must be considered.

This discussion of plumbing has been provided to prevent you from making costly plumbing mistakes—either by failure to replace inadequate or faulty plumbing, or by failure to plan the renovation to keep plumbing installation cost at a minimum. This is not to say that one plumbing line is always more economical than two. If two plumbing lines will enable you to renovate with no wall changes whereas the use of only one line would mean a complete alteration of the existing floor plan, by all means use two plumbing lines. In that case, the cost of the extra plumbing will probably be far less than substantial demolition and rebuilding. Plumbing cost must be considered in light of the total cost of renovation. However, when substantial rebuilding as well as new plumbing is required, the use of stacked back-to-back plumbing should be considered. The money saved by using one plumbing line instead of two can pay for an additional bath. The cost in relation to value received should be weighed in all decisions involving plumbing. (This is true of all other elements of a renovation also.)

Keeping costs down is necessary, but sometimes the wrong things are sacrificed in the name of the budget. People often cut out plumbing facilities they want because they think they cannot afford them. When rough plumbing (the installation of pipes inside the walls) is being done, the cost of an additional branch or two is minimal. Installing the rough plumbing does not mean that the fixtures must be installed immediately. These branches can be capped off for use at a later date. Providing new branch lines when new plumbing is being installed is relatively simple and inexpensive; doing it later involves taking the whole line apart and inserting new fittings. The cost for such a job is often prohibitive, to say nothing of the mess involved. Make provisions in the new plumbing work for future additions you may not be able to afford now. A powder room, an extra bath, a washing machine or dishwasher may be out of the question now, but if the necessary pipes are installed, they can be added easily whenever the money is available.

Any large rental apartment should have provisions for installing a washer and dryer, even if you do not supply the appliances. These facilities are a big plus in renting. So is the provision for a dishwasher. Don't forget about outside faucets, front and rear. If you are planning to buy a refrigerator with an automatic ice maker, remember to have provision made for the water such an appliance requires. Plan for a sink in the cellar if it is used for a workshop— you can use one of the old sinks that are being removed.

• GAS LINES

Gas pipes are a very small part of plumbing installation. The gas company brings the necessary gas supply into the house, and the plumber takes the job from there. Gas lines are usually needed only for stoves and gas-fired clothes dryers; the gas lines for a gas furnace are a part of heating rather than plumbing. Old houses generally have gas lines, and these can be reused if they are in the proper location and are in good condition. If gas lines are in the wrong location, it is often easier and no more expensive to disconnect the old lines and run new ones than to trace out the existing lines and reroute them.

Gas was the source of light during the Victorian era, and houses built during that time often retain evidence of the original gaslights even though the fixtures have long ago been replaced. Many renovators use the old gas lines to install gas chandeliers in living or dining room. Another common practice of renovators is the installation of gas lamps on the exterior. If you want these, remember to make provision for the installation of gas lines for the fixtures.

The gaslight age also saw wide use of gas logs in fireplaces; the vestiges of these logs can be found in pipes protruding from the floors of fireplaces and in gas shut-off valves found on the floor beside many Victorian mantels. Some people who do not want to be bothered with wood have been reviving the use of gas logs in their fireplaces.

The gas supplied to the house passes through a meter so that the gas company can bill you for the amount you use. If the house contains rental units using gas stoves, it is possible to provide separate gas meters for each apartment so that tenants pay their own gas bills. However, the amount of gas used for cooking is minimal, and an owner can often provide gas for his tenants for very little money. However, if separate gas furnaces are used in each rental unit, you should have separate gas meters.

Be sure to consider any gas requirements when planning the renovation so that necessary pipes are provided. In many homes there is no gas at all. If you do not plan to use gas but gas lines exist in the house, have the gas company remove the meter or you will be billed the monthly minimum for a service you do not use.

• ELECTRICAL WIRING

The Building Code sets standards for electrical wiring, and most cities require that new wiring be installed by licensed electricians. Just because the wiring in a house meets city requirements does not mean that it will be adequate for your needs. City regulations merely set minimum requirements that must be met in order to ensure the health and safety of residents. Current wiring may be adequate for current usage, but you may want additional equipment and appliances, and you must be sure that the wiring is adequate to service them.

The amount of electrical power available in any house depends on the *service line* that is brought to the house. The size of the service line determines the amount of electricity that can be used at any one time: the larger the service line, the more electricity available. The amount of electrical service is expressed in amperes (amps): two-hundred-amp service is larger than one-hundred-amp service, and will therefore provide more electrical power to the house. The size you need depends on your electrical requirements.

The electric company provides the service line for your house. A service line adequate fifteen years ago will scarcely be adequate for today's needs. The list of electric gadgets (toothbrushes, knives, can openers) grows each year, as do innovations such as self-defrosting refrigerators and self-cleaning electric ovens. This gradual electrification of our lives means that the average family in the United States uses many times more electricity than it did fifteen years ago.

Electric companies are aware of this rapid expansion of electrical needs and realize that older homes are not adequately wired for today's usage. For this reason, most electric companies provide some sort of *adequate-wiring survey* free of charge to property owners. This survey will determine whether the existing service is adequate for the owner's electrical requirements. If it is not, the company will determine what size service is required and will issue a report stating service size as well as the number of circuits needed inside the house and the size of wire to be used for each. This report can then be included in any contract for rewiring to ensure that all work is done in accordance with the report. Many electric companies will send out inspectors during renovation to see that adequate wiring-survey requirements have been met.

The size of the service determines the amount of electricity that can be safely used; if more power is demanded than is available, the line becomes overloaded and can cause a fire. *Fuses* are a safety device to prevent overloading. When too much power is demanded, the fuse blows and shuts off the power. *Circuit breakers* are the modern substitute for fuses. Fuses require replacement when blown; the circuit breaker merely flips off to shut off power and prevent an overload. To return power to the area, you merely flip the appropriate circuit breaker just as you would a light switch.

The service line passes through a *master circuit breaker* just after it enters the house, thereby enabling all power to be turned off at the source. The service line is then fed into a *meter* so that the electric company knows how much electricity is being used. If the house contains more than one apartment, a meter can be installed for each apartment. Separate meters allow each occupant to pay his own bill so that landlords do not have to estimate how much electricity a tenant will use when setting the rent. The tenant can then regulate how much electricity he uses and must pay for.

From the meter, wiring is divided into *circuits,* which are then carried to the various areas of the house. Each circuit has its own circuit breaker (or fuse). These circuit breakers are housed in a *circuit-breaker box,* which is installed either in the cellar or inside the apartment. (There will be at least one circuit-breaker box for each meter.) The division of wiring into circuits enables power to be turned off in one circuit without turning off power everywhere in the house. Each circuit should be clearly labeled so that you know what area it services.

It is the electrician's job to install the proper size of wire for each circuit and to divide the electrical requirements among the various circuits available, making certain that the demands made on each circuit can be met. Certain electrical equipment such as room air conditioners and electric stoves require separate lines because they use so much power, whereas several lights or plugs can be placed on the same line. It is mandatory to give your electrician all of your electrical requirements in advance of rewiring so that he can plan his installation properly. One renovator forgot to tell the electrician that he was planning to use an electric stove; when the stove arrived, it could not be installed.

If a professional inspection of the house was made, you will have a report on the condition of the existing wiring in the house. If the wiring is safe (that is, the existing circuits are not overloaded) but inadequate to supply all of your needs, it is often possible merely to add to the wiring already present. This can be done even when the size of the service must be changed in order to install new circuits. Bringing in a new service line involves no work on the wiring inside the house.

You may have a problem reusing existing wiring when separate meters are to replace the one currently in use. Let us give a simple example to illustrate the point:

A two-story house currently has one meter. A renovation of the house will create two apartments, one on each floor of the house, and each apartment is to have its own meter. The existing wiring is good, but it must be separated and fed into the appropriate meter. If the wiring was installed so that each circuit only supplied electricity to one floor, there is no problem. If, however, one circuit supplied electricity to parts of both floors, the separation of wiring is difficult.

Tracing out existing wiring is often arduous and time-consuming. Many electricians will refuse to do the job if it is a complex one. Tracing the existing wiring to reuse it may be just as expensive as disconnecting it and running all new wires.

Electrical work involves running wires inside the walls and ceilings. These wires are run into *electrical boxes* to which switches, outlets, fixtures, and special electrical appliances are attached. Where existing plaster is to remain, the job involves breaking small holes and snaking the wires inside, and making holes large enough to house boxes at specified locations. Where new partitions are being erected, installing new wiring is a simple matter. Since more time is involved in snaking wires inside of existing walls than in running wires in open partitions, electricians often charge more for the former. Therefore, all necessary wiring should be done at the beginning of renovation rather than after new walls have been closed up and existing ones patched and painted.

Renovators are generally more familiar with the need for adequate wiring, possibly because of the fire hazard of old electrical systems, than they are with the need for adequate plumbing, but often they do not carefully study their electrical needs when planning the renovation.

The planning of wiring is essential, but the renovator seldom realizes its importance until he suddenly discovers that there is no outlet in the bathroom for his electric razor or that the walk-in closet is unusable because it has no light.

Electricians often charge by the box—so much for each outlet, switch, fixture, and so on. The cost can mount rapidly, so keep it in mind when planning, but do not cut corners where you may regret it.

- OUTLETS

There are three types of electrical outlets: *convenience outlets,* the regular kind of double plug used for lamps, radios, and other small appliances; *utility outlets* for kitchens, workshops, and other areas where appliances drawing a lot of current are used; and *heavy-duty outlets* for such equipment as air conditioners, electric stoves, and electric dryers. Several convenience outlets can be placed on one circuit, whereas utility and heavy-duty outlets require their own lines, with heavy-duty outlets requiring the use of heavier wire than the other two.

The first thing you must consider is how many outlets of each variety you will need. Most electrical codes specify a minimum number of outlets for each room (according to its size and use), but you may want more. Next consider their location. You may have a sufficient number of outlets, but if they are not properly located, they can be frustrating. Consider the following when planning outlets:

1. Outlets should be no farther than six feet apart, because that is the standard length of appliance and light cords.
2. Provide enough outlets in the kitchen for all your appliances—then add another for future acquisitions.
3. Do not forget about outlets in the bathroom.
4. If the cellar is to be a work area, provide outlets there too, although they can be added later since exposed wires there are not a problem.
5. Provide outlets at the top and bottom of stairs and in or near halls for vacuum cleaning.
6. Wire for dishwasher, washing machine, and dryer even though you do not plan to install them immediately.
7. Do not forget to add weatherproof exterior outlets in the garden.
8. Wire for gadgets such as timer, light, and clock on stove; this line is different from the one that provides electricity for oven and burners, and must also be provided for gas stoves with such equipment.
9. There are outlets with special covers to protect children: Consider these if there are toddlers in your house.
10. Many building codes now require an air conditioning outlet in every room when central air conditioning is not being installed. If this regulation does not apply in

your area, it is a good idea to consider it anyway unless the climate precludes the need.

- ## FIXTURES

The next consideration is the placement of fixtures. Fixtures are either surface-mounted on wall or ceiling, or recessed. In surface mounting, only the electrical box is recessed; but in recessed fixtures, the fixture must also be inside the wall or ceiling, and a wooden frame to hold it must be made and put in place by the carpenter before the electrician installs the fixture. Location of recessed fixtures depends on the position of beams. Beams normally run the width of the house, and there is less space between them in old houses than in new ones. It takes several recessed fixtures to give as much light as many surface-mounted fixtures using the same size bulb. Recessed lighting can be extremely effective, but you should be aware of the added installation cost (more fixtures required to produce enough light, extra cost of framing out) before deciding to use it. Also think twice about putting many recessed fixtures in a twelve-foot ceiling if you mind getting out a tall stepladder whenever a light bulb needs replacing. Recessed lights are ideal for low ceilings, where surface-mounted ceiling fixtures make ceilings seem even lower.

There are two kinds of light bulbs used in fixtures: fluorescent and incandescent. Fluorescent bulbs are more economical, and bulbs last far longer, but this kind of lighting is so often associated with institutions and unattractive fixtures that many renovators do not consider it. There are, however, very attractive surface-mounted and recessed fixtures available for use in bathrooms and kitchens. Strip fluorescent lights can be used effectively when concealed under kitchen cabinets or used behind decorative moldings around the ceiling of any room. Another attractive solution is to conceal fluorescent strips behind translucent fiberglass panels. An entire fiberglass ceiling can be hung in baths and kitchens that have ceiling heights of ten feet or more. Seal all holes and cracks, leave pipes along the ceiling exposed (or do not bother to recess new ones). Paint the ceiling all white to reflect light, install enough fluorescent strips to give proper light, and then hang the luminous ceiling (metal strips hold the fiberglass panels). These can be installed by a handy homeowner and are available from Sears Roebuck or your local supply house. The effect is of a skylit room, and the bulbs last a year or more without replacing.

The exact location of all fixtures must be known when the electrician does his wiring, so that boxes can be installed in the proper places. Adequate lighting is difficult to achieve, as most of us are sadly aware. In a renovation, you have an opportunity to remedy the situation. Take the time to plan it properly. You may even want to consult a lighting expert. At any rate, be sure to consider the following:

1. Although specific fixtures (except those that are recessed) need not be selected at the time the location of electrical boxes is planned, the kind of fixture to be used may influence the location, particularly in wall-mounted types, where the size of the fixture may determine its placement.
2. Fixtures using several candelabra-type bulbs are lovely, but changing the bulbs, each of which inevitably burns out at a different time, can be a real nuisance. Limit the use of such fixtures for sanity's sake.
3. The location of the ceiling fixture in a dining room can be critical, since most people want it centered over the dining table. If there is any doubt about the location of the table or if you contemplate shifting its location occasionally, you may want to omit the overhead fixture and instead use wall fixtures with candles on the table.
4. If you plan to use heavy chandeliers or ceiling fixtures, be sure to let your contractor know so that he can make

any necessary provisions. An electrical box will not carry the load of a heavy fixture—usually a pipe or small beam must be put in to support the weight.

5. Do not forget about lights for the cellar, attic, and inside closets.

6. Lights should be provided for the exterior of the building, both front and rear. If an extension roof is used for a terrace, put a light there, too. If the house has a high stoop, you may want a light at the top of the stoop as well as at the ground floor entrance.

7. Electricians often object to drilling through masonry walls, and will run exposed exterior wires to avoid it. Insist that no wires be run along the exterior of your house even if it does cost extra to recess them, so that exposed conduit does not detract from the beauty of the façade.

8. If you want a gaslight in front of your house, provision must be made by the plumber.

· SWITCHES

Once you have located all fixtures in the house, you can plan the location of switches controlling them. Some observation of your current residence will start your thinking in the right direction. Have you ever lived in a place where the bathroom light switch was behind the door, so that you had to go into the dark room and partially close the door before you could turn on the light? Or have you found light switches placed so high that your children had to be seven or eight years old before they could reach them? Sometimes this can be an advantage, but more often it is a nuisance. Whatever you want, plan deliberately, so that you will not have to live with the accidental whim of the electrician. Architect Benjamin Kitchen, designing his own Philadelphia town house, put the switch by the front door low enough so that it could be turned on with his knee when he came home loaded with packages As soon as all new partitions are erected, mark the exact position of each outlet and switch so that there can be no doubt about where you want them to be. Insist that all switches and outlets be placed at the same height and absolutely vertical, or you may find yourself with some absurd variations.

One switch can control one or more fixtures. Sometimes it is pointless to have a switch for each fixture. On the other hand, you want to be able to control the number of lights illuminated at one time, so that four lights do not go on when only one is needed. In some cases you should be able to turn lights on and off at more than one location: this can be done with three-way switches. You will probably want three-way switches at the top and bottom of all stairs and possibly at either end of large rooms. It is even possible to control lights all over the house from a central location, such as the master bedroom or front door. Remember however, that when you pay by the electrical box, a switch is separate from the fixture it controls, and a three-way switch counts as three boxes.

When planning switches, consider the following:

1. Dimmer switches can be used in living and dining room to alter the intensity of light. There is an additional charge for these, and if money is tight, they can be installed later by a handy homeowner familiar with wiring. There is no appreciable saving in electricity when lights are dimmed.

2. The budget-conscious renovator should be aware of the combination outlet, where switch and outlet are installed for the price of only one box. However, you get only one outlet, so do not use it where you may have two appliances in constant use, such as an electric toothbrush and an electric razor. This type of outlet is ideal for a guest bath or powder room.

3. Exterior lights can be controlled by a photoelectric cell that automatically turns on lights at night, especially convenient for those who often return home after dark.

Photoelectric cells are sometimes activated by shadows, or on cloudy days: this must be considered in chosing their location. Another solution is to connect exterior lights to an automatic timer.
4. Closet lights can be operated by an old-fashioned pull-chain or switches that automatically turn on the light when the door opens and off when the door shuts.

• OTHER WIRING

Another electrical system that should be considered is an *intercom*. Many urban apartment dwellers are accustomed to the convenience of being able to ask who is calling when the front doorbell rings without going downstairs to answer it. These systems can be equally important to a house that has more than two floors, and can be useful inside the house to communicate with family members who are several floors away. An adequate system need not be prohibitively expensive, and should be included in your wiring plans.

Another idea borrowed from the apartment house is the installation of a *door buzzer system*, used to let visitors into a locked building. When combined with an intercom, the buzzer system can save the homeowner countless steps, because he can release the lock merely by pushing a button at the intercom box. The location of intercom boxes and door buzzers is important. There should be at least one on every floor, located so that it is easily accessible. Do not forget the cellar if it is a work area; the one on the entrance floor is more useful at the rear than close to the entrance. Be sure that intercoms are placed at the proper height for the family—better too low than too high. This system is virtually a necessity where rental units are on top floors of four-story and five-story houses.

In summation, a rewiring job should include the following items where applicable:

1. New service line from the street
2. New meters when more than one meter is used
3. Replacement of fuses with circuit breakers
4. A circuit-breaker box inside each apartment
5. Adequate and properly located outlets, fixtures, and switches
6. Air conditioning outlets or electrical wiring for a central system
7. Heavy duty lines for electric stoves and other appliances
8. Wiring for heating and air conditioning thermostats
9. Wiring for dishwashers, washing machines, and clothes dryers
10. Intercom and door-buzzer systems
11. Wiring for special requirements, such as a central stereo system

For a discussion of preparing and reading electrical plans, see pages 223 and 228.

• *Prewiring for Telephones and Cable Television.* Telephones require wiring also. In old houses a maze of wires is often found around door and window moldings, along baseboards, and on the exterior of the house. These wires are telephone installations that have accumulated over the years. Telephone installers usually find it necessary to put in new wires with each installation, but they seldom, if ever, remove those no longer in use. The need for so many exposed wires can be greatly reduced or eliminated altogether by *prewiring for telephones* during renovation. When the walls are open during construction, telephone wires can be placed inside. Telephone wires must run from a box that provides the service to each location in the house where a telephone is desired. In prewiring, these lines are run through the house vertically and horizontally, and connecting blocks (those square plastic boxes from which installations of individual phones are made) are located on each floor. Any installation is then made from these blocks without requiring wires to be brought all the way from the telephone box. If the exact location of telephones is determined in the renovation planning, it is possible to have the connecting blocks placed in the exact location where they are needed when prewiring is done. Remember to consider the location of phones in the back yard or cellar workshop, unless you plan to use a cordless phone in such areas.

The location of the telephone box can often be a problem to homeowners. In New York, for instance, not every house has a box, because many different lines are fed through one box. If yours is a row house and the telephone box is in your back yard, the repair man may have to troop in and out of your house to make repairs on any phone serviced by the box. Having the box located in the cellar instead of the back yard can save wear and tear on your house as well as your nerves, particularly in bad weather. Your local telephone company should be contacted about the relocation of the box as well as about the availability of prewiring. Prewiring is only done where the necessary walls will be open.

The demand for telephone service has increased so rapidly that in many areas there is a delay in installation, or in getting a phone number assigned. It is a good idea to reserve your phone in advance to be sure you get it when you need it.

If you plan to use cable television, the necessary wiring should be done during construction so that these wires can also be hidden in the walls.

· HEATING

There are three kinds of central heating systems in use in older city houses: forced air, steam, and hot water. Each of these systems requires a furnace, which is generally fired by either oil or gas, although coal-fired furnaces are sometimes still in use. Steam and hot-water systems usually require radiators—steam or hot water is produced by the furnace and moves through pipes to the radiators. In forced-air systems, heated air moves through metal ducts to outlets (registers) in the floor or walls of each room. The ducts for forced-air systems can also be used for air conditioning.

Many older homes that had no central heating systems are now heated by gas space heaters, either free standing or installed in fireplaces. These can be extremely dangerous if not properly ventilated or if not in good working order. Electric space heaters can also be found in some homes, particularly in the South where winters are mild. The advantage of space heaters is that you need heat only those areas in use. Because the cost of a new heating system is substantial, many renovators use these space heaters until they can afford new systems. If you are doing this, be sure to have heaters checked thoroughly to see that they are properly ventilated and have no gas leaks.

Before you make any decision about a heating system, you should determine the condition of the one that currently exists: it may be in good condition. If it works, leave well enough alone. You may have problems with a new one. Old furnaces may need attachments added to make them easier to operate, but such work is minor.

Often pipes and radiators or ducts are in good condition but the furnace is old and inefficient (that is, burns too much fuel for the amount of heat produced). If so, you need only replace the furnace. The price of a new furnace is small compared to the cost of a whole new heating system. Furnaces can sometimes be converted to use another fuel (coal to oil, or oil to gas) without having to install a new furnace.

Old-fashioned radiators are not the most attractive things, but they can often be cleverly camouflaged, recessed, or even replaced with the newer baseboard type of radiation. People can often learn to live with radiators and exposed heating pipes when they learn the price of installing a new heating system.

However, there are times when a new system makes sense. If the existing system does not provide sufficient heat for the house, you must change the system if you cannot expand the current one to supply demand. If you are installing central air conditioning with ductwork, it may make sense to use the same ducts to supply heat, which will enable you to get rid of the old radiators and exposed heating pipes.

When deciding on a new heating system you may want to consider electric heat. There is one big drawback: in most areas electrical rates are high in comparison with other fuels, and the house must be well insulated if costs are to be kept at a reasonable level. In addition, electric heat is not as hot as gas heat. The air emitted by a gas-fired forced air system is hotter than the air emitted by an electric forced-air system. However, electric heat is much cleaner than gas or oil heat, and an electric furnace does not have to be vented.

When selecting the type of system to install, you should consider not only installation and operating costs, but also be sure that there are competent people to install and service the system. The following example, though not a case of new installation, illustrates this point:

Carol and Larry Hulack bought a house in Manhattan that had a hot-water heating system. The engineer who checked the house praised the condition of the system and told them how lucky they were to have hot-water heat. The

Hulacks were delighted, until the renovation was finished. They could not get any hot water until the furnace was turned on since the hot water was provided by a heating coil on the furnace. The plumber could not make the furnace work. After a week of bathing in cold water, they found someone who knew something about hot-water heating systems. They were well into the winter before the system was made to function properly, not because anything was wrong with the system, but because hot-water heat is rare in Manhattan and not many people understand how it works.

The same is true of gas furnaces. In Manhattan most furnaces are oil fired, and therefore many people service the equipment. It is more difficult to find someone to service a gas furnace, because the gas company, unlike fuel oil companies, provides only fuel. Although Brooklyn Union Gas gives its customers free service, Con Edison, serving Manhattan, provides no service at all.

If you install a new heating system, carefully select the person who designs it. He should be familiar with the peculiar features of old houses, the cost of installing and operating (in old houses rather than new ones) each type of system, and the availability of service for each. Before you let anyone design your heating system, check on him as thoroughly as you would an architect. (See page 237 on checking an architect.) If your architect is to design the system, be sure he is qualified to do so. As for the person who will install it, check him as carefully as you would a general contractor (see pages 252–55), and be sure he gives an adequate guarantee of the work.

Because of the difficulty of installing ducts in an existing house, it often makes sense to install more than one system. In a two-story house you might have a furnace for each floor, or one furnace for the living areas and another for the sleeping areas. It is obviously more expensive to buy an additional furnace, but if less damage to walls and ceilings is needed to install two separate systems, it might be preferable. Sometimes it is the only way to heat an old house properly, and can prove more economical because you only have to heat or cool space that is in use.

It is worth considering separate heating systems for rental units: tenants can then regulate the temperature to suit their needs. And it is ideal for four- and five-story row houses where the ground floor may be too hot while the top floor is too cold.

• AIR CONDITIONING

Air conditioning, once considered a luxury, is rapidly becoming so prevalent that many people take it for granted, and many building codes require installation of air conditioning outlets when rewiring. Air conditioning can be provided by individual window units or installation of a central system. In either case, there must be adequate electrical service to the house and electric lines inside the house to service it.

Window units are far cheaper than a central system when only one or two are needed. However, if very many window units are required, you should compare their cost (plus cost of necessary wiring) with the cost of a central system. If the cost is close, the central system is preferable.

Since central air conditioning requires a network of ducts that usually should be hidden in the walls, they must be installed during the early part of the renovation, while walls are still open. If you have a forced-air heating system, the ducts can sometimes be used to service central air conditioning by simply adding the necessary equipment or replacing the furnace with one designed to serve both heating and cooling. If the central system must be designed from scratch, it should be designed by an air conditioning specialist. Two sets of ducts (one to circulate cool air and the other to remove warmer air) are needed, and they must be located so that an even temperature is maintained throughout each room as well as throughout the house. Locating ducts within the framework of a house where floor joists (beams) and partitions are in place before the system is designed is much more difficult than when the system is a part of the design of a new house. Make sure that whoever designs your air conditioning system is familiar with the problems of installation in old houses.

If the cost of a central air conditioning system is more than your budget will allow, it is possible to install ducts and necessary wiring during the renovation, postponing the purchase and installation of equipment until a later date. The cost of opening walls to install ducts later is far greater, and ducts are often difficult to locate properly because of pipes, etc., inside. The installation of central air conditioning is almost a matter of now or never.

In an installation where more than one apartment is involved, you can have either one system for the whole house or a separate system for each apartment. The latter is obviously more expensive initially, because it involves duplicating equipment; but since tenants can pay their own air conditioning bills, the extra cost may be justified. And of course you can always provide central air conditioning for only the part of the house that you occupy.

Make certain that you thoroughly check the credentials of the person who designs and installs the air conditioning system. A guarantee of installation and equipment is mandatory.

The best heating and air conditioning systems will not work efficiently if windows, doors, and other openings are not properly sealed and caulked, and if the attic and floors above any open space under the house are not insulated. (It is not necessary to insulate a totally enclosed basement.) Proper insulation need not be a major expense. Fiberglass batting can be installed in the attic and under the house by a handy homeowner. The effective minimum thickness of insulation depends on your climate. Blown-in insulation is the only solution for houses without attic or crawl space.

The cost-effectiveness of storm windows and doors depends on the condition and type of windows and doors in the house, and the area in which it is located. Many utility companies will do an energy survey of your house free of charge and make recommendations for cost-effective changes. Income tax credits are currently allowed for money spent on insulation, weather stripping, exterior caulking, storm windows, and other energy conservation expenses. Check with your accountant or the Internal Revenue Service for specific details.

Insulating exterior walls in most old houses may not be worthwhile and is often unnecessary. An example is Martha Stamm's 1920's house in Atlanta. The house is naturally insulated with plaster on wood lath inside and brick veneer on wood sheathing on the exterior, separated by an air barrier. No further insulation is required. In fact, blown-in insulation in exterior walls could create problems, because most older houses were built without the benefit of vapor barriers, which are needed for the insulated wall.

• MECHANICAL VENTILATION

Building codes regulate the size of rooms and the amount of air each must receive. Most cities require that living rooms (any room used for living or sleeping) must have natural ventilation from windows. However, rooms such as baths and kitchens can have ventilation provided by mechanical means. Mechanical ventilation is supplied by ducts with fans attached that provide and circulate necessary air. There is either a central fan on the roof, controlled by a clock (usually located in the cellar), or individual room fans that start automatically when the light is turned on. (The building code sets requirements for mechanical ventilation—sizes of ducts and fans, installation methods, and sizes of rooms so ventilated.)

Mechanical ventilation enables the renovator to use

space that might otherwise be wasted. In the case of the row house, interior space can be used for kitchens and baths; and if the house is a deep one, this space can often provide two such rooms on each floor. (See floor plans on page 91.)

· ROOM ARRANGEMENT

As you can see, the mechanical systems in your house will affect your floor plans. The location of plumbing determines where kitchens, baths, and laundry equipment can be placed. Once you have determined the location of these rooms, you can begin to think of their size and the most desirable, convenient arrangement of other rooms in relation to them and to each other. Ideally, each room should function well within the total plan. Rooms should flow into each other so that the house has an open and spacious feeling while still providing needed privacy.

When planning room arrangement, apply all of your earlier thinking on present and future family needs and living patterns, and what you do and do not want in your house. Start thinking about details, because they must be considered when planning the location and sizes of rooms.

Think about traffic patterns when planning rooms. Avoid bottlenecks at main entrances and other areas such as halls and kitchens. There should be easy access to each room without impairing its function.

Consider the moving of furniture when planning. It is frustrating and costly to find that you must discard your sofa because you cannot get it through the door or down the hall. Halls and front doors should be three feet wide, as should doors to rooms that will have large pieces of furniture. Avoid, where possible, the use of long halls, which tend to become a maze of doors. Where a long hall is unavoidable, a width of three and a half to four feet will make it seem shorter and allow the use of decorative pieces of furniture to avoid a bowling-alley effect.

202 · *Buying and Renovating a House in the City*

Ceiling heights are an important consideration. A ten-by-fifteen-foot room with a ten-foot ceiling seems more spacious than the same room with an eight-foot ceiling. Creating wide entries, using double doors or eliminating doors altogether, helps give visual space to areas with low ceilings. On the other hand, avoid small, narrow rooms where ceilings are high, or you may have an upended-coffin effect. (Ceilings should be lowered in such areas.)

The standard-height door for today's construction is six feet eight inches or seven feet. Using these in rooms with twelve-foot ceilings, particularly when combined with original doors nine to ten feet tall, can be very disconcerting. New doors over seven feet high must be custom made and are very expensive. When old doors are not available, clever solutions can be found. Borrow from the Victorian era and install transoms (fake) above stock doors to create the illusion of height. Transoms can be solid wood painted to match the door or decorative panels, with door molding going around door and transom to the desired height.

Room sizes can be important. A living room and dining room must be large enough to accommodate needed furniture, but the use of built-in furniture can make a small room seem spacious. When the number of rooms is important and the amount of space you can afford is limited, do not rule out small rooms. One room can be divided, either permanently or temporarily, to make private areas for two children.

To make the best first impression, plan the entrance to your home so that it makes an impact. A tiny entrance hall can cause a traffic jam. Direct entrance into a major room detracts from its usefulness and subjects it to more than normal dirt and traffic. When planning the entry, remember the conveniences of coat closet and powder room for guests.

There can never be too much storage space, so be sure to plan enough. In rooms with high ceilings, utilize the space above the height of closet doors. Built-in wall cabinets or niches for open shelves can be made very easily and inexpensively between the studs in bathrooms if they are included in the plans for construction. Use the studs themselves for the sides of the cabinet or niche, with a horizontal piece for top and bottom installed at the proper height. The interior must be finished, but in most cases the sheet-rock on the wall behind can serve as the back. Add a door and molding to finish the cabinet. Old shutters make lovely doors for such cabinets and, when used on either side of the bathroom mirror, can be a custom-made detail on a very modest budget.

Pay careful attention to doors, not only their width and height but also the direction in which they open. There is nothing more annoying than having two or more doors placed close together that collide with each other, or having one open door block the use of another when the problem could be avoided by merely placing the hinge on the other side.

Think about furniture placement when planning a room arrangement. The location of doors can chop up a room or create a hall within it, making furniture arrangement difficult. Be sure that there is sufficient wall space for furniture. Sometimes it is a mistake to keep an old mantel for decorative purposes when the wall is needed for a bed, desk, or sofa.

· EQUIPMENT

When you have determined the location of all rooms, you can begin to think about plumbing fixtures, cabinets, appliances, and other items that must be selected and installed in your house. Obviously, some of these things will determine the size of rooms and should be considered when planning room arrangement. For example, if you need a lot of kitchen storage space, the kitchen must be large enough to accommodate it. However, the details of the kitchen cabinets should not be a major concern until the total floor plan of the house has been worked out. If you want the construction bids to come within your budget, choose stock (or standard) items wherever possible. Stock items can be used creatively—you don't have to pay a custom price to achieve a custom look. Clever use of inexpensive materials and equipment can create a spectacular effect. This is true of everything from doors and floors to cabinets and fixtures. White bathroom fixtures combined with distinctive wallpaper can be as attractive as colored tile and fixtures, and you have the option of changing the wallpaper when you get tired of the color. Stock kitchen cabinets can often be improved with a change of hardware. And an old dresser can become a vanity by replacing the top with formica in which a basin has been inserted. The dresser can either be stripped to the natural wood or antiqued in any number of marvelous colors.

Pay close attention to details because they can give your house a custom look. Take time to look at styles and samples of hardware, moldings, tile, and so forth well in advance of your final plans and specifications. They can be more important than you think. If you simply specify plain white tile for your bathroom floor, you may regret the choice for years if the tile man chooses to give you the unglazed type that absorbs dirt like a blotter. Think about the placement of towel bars and toilet-paper holders— trivial things that are so inconspicuous if they are right and so maddeningly annoying if they are wrong. If you think things will just appear in the proper place if left to the discretion of workmen, you may be in for an unpleasant shock.

- PLUMBING FIXTURES

You may be surprised at the infinite variety of plumbing fixtures available. There are four major plumbing fixture manufacturers (American Standard, Crane, Kohler, and Rheem) and numerous other small ones. American Standard, for instance, makes eight different styles of toilet for residential use, and each is available in a variety of colors. Plumbing fixtures consist of toilets, bidets, tubs and shower stalls, lavatories and sinks, as well as the trim (faucets and so on) that goes with them.

Each of these items should be selected and designated by manufacturer, style number, and color before the work is begun. One of the prime considerations in selecting plumbing fixtures should be their availability from local plumbing supply houses. The newest and most expensive items often require a special order, as do many colored fixtures. If a special order is necessary, it may take weeks and even months, holding up construction in the process—and the contractor may charge a higher markup for special-order material than he would for stock items. Remember that this year's fashionable color may date your bathroom five years from now, or be difficult to replace should damage occur. White fixtures are more readily available at supply houses and are less expensive than colored ones, and easy to match if replacement is needed.

All major plumbing fixture manufacturers have showrooms in New York, Chicago, and other large cities. You can write to them for brochures and catalogues of all their equipment or get the information from local supply houses.

Some city building codes do not allow the use of certain plumbing equipment, such as garbage disposals. Be sure to check city regulations before ordering. Your architect, plumber, or plumbing supply house should know, but a call to the building department is always wise.

Bathtubs come in two heights, fourteen inches and sixteen inches. The fourteen-inch tub is the cheaper builder's model and is ideal for small children who have difficulty stepping over the additional two inches and for those who prefer showers, for the same reason. However, for people who like to soak, the sixteen-inch tub is preferable. If the

Bathrooms like this are a familiar sight to renovators (sometimes there are as many as six or eight in one house). New plumbing fixtures, taste, and imagination can transform them.

exact tub is not specified, the contractor may install the builder's model to save money.

Standard rectangular tubs are five feet long. (Tubs are available in five-and-a-half- and six-foot lengths, but they are expensive and usually require a special order.) Modern tubs are normally recessed into a niche and are finished

along only one side; you must specify which side is to be finished. If the end of the tub is to be exposed because it is fitted into a corner instead of a niche, you must buy one with a finished end.

Fiberglass tubs are replacing enameled cast iron tubs as standard equipment in most houses. They are less expensive and much lighter in weight. They usually come with molded wall panels, thereby eliminating the need for tiled walls and caulking between tub and wall which needs frequent replacement. A few cautions about using fiberglass tubs: the surface is easily scratched and stained, and cannot be cleaned with abrasive scouring powder. Furthermore, the tubs with molded walls are sometimes too large to move into the house through doorways and other narrow areas. Lastly, unless some insulation is placed behind the walls and around the tub, the noise level is high when water hits the fiberglass surface.

Always install a shower body in at least one tub, even if you do not take showers. Its cost is nominal, and it will add to the value of your house. On the other hand, have at least one tub in the house even if you always take showers, for the same reason. If you plan your plumbing facilities exclusively for your own idiosyncracies, you may have difficulty selling, when and if that day should come.

Lavatories are made of enameled cast iron or vitreous china. There are pros and cons for each type—enameled cast iron chips, and china cracks. It is not a good idea to use china lavatories in children's areas.

Most lavatories come in a variety of sizes and shapes, in wall-hung, freestanding, and counter-top models. Be sure that at least one lavatory in the house is large enough for washing lingerie, hose, and other items.

There are two kinds of installation for counter-top lavatories, one for formica tops and another for marble. You must specify the type of installation when ordering the lavatory in order to get the proper fixture. In addition, counter tops and basins molded in one piece are available in Corian, a man-made material with the appearance of marble, which can be cut with a saw. Corian is also available in sheets for kitchen counters as well as one-piece counters with molded sinks. This product should not be confused with cultured marble, a less expensive product, which cannot be scoured and is subject to chipping, cracking, and crazing.

Many toilets come in standard and elongated models. Be sure the room can handle the additional length when ordering the latter for a small bathroom. Wall-hung toilets are becoming popular, but special provision must be made for reinforcing the wall that carries their weight. Toilets do not usually come equipped with seats, so be sure to order them.

Most plumbing fixtures do not come equipped with trim (faucets and so on), so this must be selected separately. The new single lever and push-pull faucets are becoming popular, but remember that they are difficult for small children to operate.

A wide variety of shower heads is available. Those with adjustable head and spray are worth the slight additional cost. There are even thermostatic controls that can be installed on the shower body, enabling the bather to set water temperature and have it maintained. For real luxury, you can have a shower body installed at both ends of the tub so that the backside does not get cold while the frontside is warm.

• KITCHEN CABINETS AND COUNTER TOPS

There is infinite variety in both the design and cost of kitchen cabinets, from mail-order catalogue to custom cabinetmaker. You can order stock, ready-made cabinets and have your contractor or carpenter install them. Or you can go to a kitchen planning center, which will help you design your kitchen, sell you what you need, and install everything. And if stock cabinets do not appeal to you, you

Inexpensive stock cabinets, a butcher-block counter top, and economy vinyl floor combined with original brick hearth in Stanforth kitchen (facing page). Many renovators have converted shabby rooms like this one (shown on this page) into attractive kitchens.

can hire a carpenter or cabinetmaker to build your cabinets exactly to your liking. Most stock cabinets do not come with counter tops—those must be provided separately. Formica counter tops can have edges finished with metal strips or be self-edged; you must specify which you prefer. Butcher-block counter tops, usually of maple, are a great asset to any kitchen, allowing you to chop and cut at random. They can be installed in special areas or used for every counter top. Or if you prefer, you can have counter tops made of ceramic tile.

Back splashes are normally part of the counter top, and their height must be specified. With back splashes more than six inches high, you may want to have electrical outlets recessed into them. The outlet can be installed the usual way, or with plugs side by side instead of one above the other. If you have self-edged backsplashes, you may want to use plugmold mounted on top of your backsplash to provide outlets. Plugmold is a metal channel which houses electrical outlets at regular intervals (you must specify the outlet spacing when ordering). Plugmold is 1½" wide and ¾" deep (the same depth as most backsplashes). Plugmold with outlet spacing every twelve inches allows you to have a plug wherever you might need it along the length of your counter. It is a bit more expensive than regular outlets, but the convenience is worth the additional expense. The plugmold can be painted to match the counter top or the wall. The color of plugmold blends nicely with the color of wood in a butcher-block counter.

If an existing counter top is stained or badly scratched, or if you just can't abide the color, there may be an alternative to tearing out the counter and replacing it. If the Formica is firmly attached to its plywood base, it is possible to glue new Formica onto the existing counter, if counter and backsplash are self-edged.

When using stock cabinets, you can seldom buy them to fit your space exactly. Filler pieces to match wooden cabinets are used in the spaces between cabinets and walls. Be sure to order these filler pieces when you order cabinets. When selecting cabinets, think about such features as adjustable shelves in overhead cabinets, roll-out shelves in base cabinets, and drawers on rollers. If your kitchen has high ceilings, you may want two sets of overhead cabinets installed one above the other for maximum storage space. The top cabinets can store seldom-used items.

It is possible to give your kitchen a face-lift without replacing all the cabinets. By merely changing the cabinet doors you can transform your kitchen at a fraction of the cost of cabinet replacement, even if you must have the new doors custom-made. Another alternative is to remove all overhead cabinet doors and paint the remaining cabinets for an open look.

· APPLIANCES

Everybody is familiar with appliances, even people who have never bought one. Every city is full of appliance dealers. *Consumer Reports* regularly gives ratings to the various models, and you might want to check their back issues before making your selection. Be sure to purchase appliances easily serviced during the warranty period because a guaranteee means nothing if there is no service by the manufacturer in your area.

The cost of appliances is directly related to the number of gadgets they contain. A "stripped down" stove is often half the price of the same stove with automatic timer, rotisserie, and other options. If your budget is tight, consider the cost of extra features in relation to their usefulness before deciding you need them. Also, when a new model first comes out, it is usually more expensive than one that has been in use for some time.

Do some window shopping and comparative pricing before selecting your appliances. (If you have several apartments, you may be able to get a discount from a dealer-distributor. Ask.) You should have the manufacturer's model number of every appliance you have selected. And remember to check the measurements of each appliance to be sure it will fit into the space allocated for it and can be moved through doorways and up or down stairs where necessary.

Wall ovens and counter-top burners take more space than a regular stove and limit counter area. There are regular stoves (forty inches wide, as opposed to the standard thirty- and thirty-six-inch models) with two ovens and six burners. If you like to cook and the size of your kitchen is limited, consider one of these. Another solution for those who want two ovens and more than four burners is to buy two apartment-size stoves. These are twenty inches wide and provide ovens adequate for cooking even the largest turkeys. You have the option of chosing one gas and one electric stove if you so desire.

Built-in dishwashers normally do not come with a front panel; it must be ordered separately. You can have one made to match your cabinets.

Refrigerator doors can be hinged on either the right or left. To prevent having the door open against a counter instead of a wall, be sure to specify which you want. In some refrigerators, particularly side-by-side models, the doors must swing open 180° before drawers nearest the door can be removed. This means that such refrigerators cannot be installed with sides against a wall. Also, don't forget that refrigerators with icemakers must have water. This is usually no problem, but be sure to plan for it.

Refrigerator sizes are expressed in cubic feet, which tells you nothing about the width, height, and depth of the appliance. Be sure to check dimensions so that the refrigerator fits into your kitchen.

It is often difficult to find space for a washing machine and dryer. The appliances that fit one on top of the other (stacked units) are often the answer, because they can be placed in a small, deep closet. Remember that dryers must be vented.

· DECORATING

"Decorating" is used here to describe that part of renovation related to interior decoration—painting, flooring, lighting fixtures, hardware, and other miscellaneous items. This stage of the planning is so much fun for most people that they fail to recognize the importance of what goes before.

All decorating is a matter of taste. What pleases me does not necessarily please you. Our only concern in this area is to point out the practical considerations to be taken into account. One that is often overlooked is maintenance. A white vinyl floor may be ever so lovely when laid, but the job of keeping it spotless is endless.

Cost is another consideration. Be sure that you get a dollar's worth of value for every dollar you spend. It is often possible to achieve the same look for a lower price if you are willing to spend some time looking at products and thinking about the desired effect.

If you are having difficulty making a decision, let it wait for a while. You can hardly do without a refrigerator; but if your kitchen is not painted for a time, it will not interfere with normal living. Better to wait than to be sorry.

· CITY REGULATIONS AFFECTING RENOVATION

Just because you plan to do a renovation does not mean that you are free to do whatever you choose. Each city has rules and regulations designed to protect its citizens. The two basic areas of concern are (1) zoning laws and (2) building codes. Any new construction or renovation of existing structures falls under the jurisdiction of both areas, and the renovator must acquaint himself in advance with these regulations to be sure he is not breaking the law.

- BUILDING CODES

Building codes vary from city to city, but each city has one. The building code is the compilation of all laws relating to building (new construction, alteration of existing conditions, and maintenance). These regulations have been passed over the years in order to ensure the health and safety of citizens.

The renovator must find out how the local building code affects the work he intends to do. You need the answers to the following questions (if you plan to use an architect or a general contractor, he should know; if not, phone the building department):

1. Must plans be filed with and approved by the city?
2. Is a building permit necessary?
3. Does the city require the use of licensed contractors?
4. Does the city inspect the work?
5. Is a certificate of occupancy or a certificate of completion required when the work is complete?

Many renovators do not adhere to building code regulations, either because they are ignorant of them or because they do not want to be bothered. Failure to comply with the building code is never a good idea—the penalty for getting caught is not worth the risk. City regulations concerning approval of work, permits, inspections, and so on are all very valid. The city wants to ensure that all buildings are structurally sound and free of fire and health hazards. These regulations protect you against faulty work and are written for your benefit. To ignore them is to leave yourself wide open for problems.

- APPROVAL OF PLANS

Not all renovation work requires the submission of plans to the building department. Generally, city approval is required when there are wall changes or a change in occupancy (the number or composition of apartments). City approval is usually required for any new plumbing, wiring, or any other change affected by building code regulations.

The filing (submission) of plans is often required where city approval must be obtained, and approval must be obtained before any work is started. If the only changes to be made are plumbing and wiring, the contractor doing the work can file the necessary papers with the building department. If there are to be structural changes (removal or addition of walls) or a change in the number of apartments, a set of floor plans often must be filed. In some cities, like New York and Chicago, these plans must be stamped by a licensed architect or professional engineer. In other cities, like Washington, plans can be drawn and filed by either the owner or the contractor.

Codes vary so from city to city that you will have to find out what is pertinent in your area. However, do not work without needed city approval. If a city inspector discovers illegal work in progress, he can shut down the job as well as impose a fine. An owner should doubt the honesty of any contractor willing to do work illegally: Is he trying to get away with improper work?

Although the city may never realize that illegal work has been done, the owner may have problems if he wants to sell a house that has been altered illegally. An astute lawyer will insist that a house his client purchases is a legal residence. Trying to obtain approval after the fact can often be difficult and sometimes impossible. Why take a chance?

· BUILDING PERMITS

Building permits are generally required for any alteration and are issued only after any necessary city approval. The building permit, which usually must be displayed on the premises while construction is in progress, is certification that work is being done. The job is recorded, and inspectors are usually sent out to see that work complies with the building code.

Building permits are obtained at a nominal fee from the department of buildings by the owner, architect, or contractor. It is generally better to have one of the latter get the permit, since he is familiar with the procedure. There are instances when permits are necessary but filing of plans is not needed. In such cases, the risks involved in not obtaining a permit are the same as those for not filing plans.

• LICENSED CONTRACTORS

Generally, new plumbing and electrical work must be performed by men licensed in those trades. A few cities even require the licensing of general contractors. These contractors are familiar with the building code and risk losing their licenses if the work is not performed properly. (Plumbers and electricians do not have to be licensed to do repair and maintenance work.) Licensed contractors know they must obtain permits and will usually be sure they have all necessary approvals before they start work.

In some cities licensed tradesmen sell the use of their licenses so that nonlicensed men can do the work. Martha Stamm had an experience with an unlicensed plumber working with a borrowed license. The man was not familiar with new installations and, furthermore, did not know how to read floor plans. When plumbing pipes began appearing in strange places, Martha got very upset. It was then that she learned that he was using someone's else's license. He was thrown off the job, and the new plumber had to replace practically all the work that had been done. There was a loss of time and money, to say nothing of the annoyance to the owners. Such an experience points out the hazards of using unlicensed plumbers and electricians.

- CITY INSPECTION

The building department has a staff of inspectors whose job it is to inspect new construction and renovation as well as the conditions in existing structures. Often the inspectors are put in charge of one specific trade, such as plumbing, electrical, or plastering. How often and by how many inspectors a renovation must be checked will depend on the city's policy, but each job requiring a permit must usually be inspected at least once. Many cities require the inspectors to approve the job when it is complete.

Building inspectors can be terribly helpful and cooperative, or they can be a nuisance. In some cities it is the deplorable custom to give "gifts" to inspectors in order to make life easier for everyone. When this is expected and not forthcoming, the building inspector can make life miserable by finding endless faults with the work.

- CERTIFICATE OF OCCUPANCY

The certificate of occupancy (C.O.) is a document given by the city at the completion of construction, certifying that the house complies with all building department regulations and is ready for occupancy. This document may also be called a certificate of inspection, a certificate of completion, or any of various other names. Some cities issue no document at the end of the job. If, however, such a document is part of city procedure, it is mandatory that the owner obtain it, since it certifies the work as legal and prevents later problems. In the case of new construction or the creation of new apartments, a C.O. is often required before the house or apartments can be occupied. Inspectors can force people to move out when no C.O. has been obtained. Why take this risk?

Take the time to find out about zoning regulations and building codes in advance of making final plans. "But I didn't know . . ." will not solve problems brought about by ignorance or failure to comply with the law. Zoning regulations control the use of land: the size of the building, its placement on the lot, the use of the building and the site. Zoning can have serious implications for the renovator. These regulations can prevent creating a rental unit in your house, preclude additions to your house, prevent converting commercial property to residential use, and deny you use of space in your house for an office. It is imperative that you check zoning regulations before purchasing a piece of property. Although it is possible to get zoning changed on a single property or a whole area, or to get a variance, the procedure is lengthy and the chance of success is questionable. If a zoning change is required, discuss the matter in detail with a knowledgeable attorney or with your city zoning department.

This unusual double octagon house (dubbed "The Folly") in the Columbus Historic District is a National Historic Landmark. It has been lovingly restored by Clason Kyle, who has had no difficulty finding tenants who appreciate living in an architectural gem.

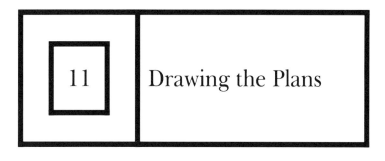

11 Drawing the Plans

THE PURPOSE OF floor plans is to put down onto paper a picture of the house as it should be when finished, so that contractor and workmen will know what walls to remove, what to leave, and what to build. If plans are accurate and detailed, there can be no mistake about where things are to be located and what must be done. Many renovations have been done without floor plans; some have been successful, others have had problems that could have been prevented by a set of plans. You must understand all about floor plans before determining whether you need them and whether you should hire an architect or do the plans and other architectural work yourself.

The best way to start planning your renovation is to obtain a set of floor plans of the house as it exists when you buy it. These are often available from the building department. You can ask the seller to supply you with a set or go down and check what is on file yourself. (If you want to get plans of a building you do not yet own, you generally must have a letter of authorization from the owner.) You can either trace the plans or have the city make a copy for you for a nominal charge. Make sure the plans you have are accurate. Measure actual room sizes, and compare them to the plans according to the scale indicated. (The most common scale used is a quarter of an inch to each foot.) If plans of the house as it presently exists are not available, have some made by a competent draftsman or your architect.

Floor plans not only show room sizes, but also the relationship of one room to another. You may have difficulty visualizing a decrepit bathroom free of fixtures and tile and converted into a small study or guest room. With plans of the existing house you will be able to see rooms in perspective without being prejudiced by their current condition.

Scale rulers (available at stationery stores) are very useful in reading and making floor plans: You do not have to translate inches into feet—the ruler does that for you. Also available are scale templates (stencils for bathroom fixtures, kitchen cabinets, appliances, and furniture). By drawing a bed or chair on a floor plan, you can get a feeling for the size of a room.

It is mandatory that you become familiar with floor plans and know how to understand them. This is true whether or not you are having an architect design your renovation: you want to be sure that the plans include everything you had in mind.

A complete set of floor plans should provide the following information:

1. The location of all walls (those to remain, to be removed, and to be built)
2. The location and size of all windows
3. The location and size of all doors and the way they are hinged
4. The location of all plumbing fixtures
5. The exact size of all rooms and closets
6. The location of all stairs

7. The location of plumbing lines, radiators, fireplaces, cabinets, appliances, mechanical ventilation and air conditioning ducts, and wiring

In addition, the floor plans can contain a *finish schedule* that gives information about floors, walls, ceilings, and so forth. The simple finish schedule on the next page was used for the renovation of a New York City brownstone.

Most city house renovations do not require elaborate floor plans (plans are usually two or three pages), but the plans for complex renovations can run ten pages or more. The plans for a simple renovation can include electrical requirements on the floor plan, but more complex jobs should have a separate set of electrical plans. Electrical plans are simply a set of floor plans, minus all written details, that show the location of each switch, outlet, fixture, intercom, or other electrical device. The following electrical symbols are used on floor plans:

ELECTRICAL SYMBOLS

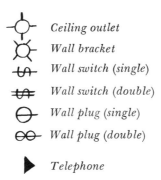

Ceiling outlet

Wall bracket

Wall switch (single)

Wall switch (double)

Wall plug (single)

Wall plug (double)

Telephone

It is often impossible to get enough detail on floor plans to give workmen information needed to do the proper job. In such cases, *detail drawings* may be necessary. Details may be shown of custom bookcases, a fireplace to be built, or a kitchen with exact dimensions of cabinets and appliances

Finish Schedule

AREA	FLOOR	WALLS	CEILING	CEILING HEIGHT	REMARKS
Hall	carpet	repair existing	existing plaster	8'6"	repair existing floor for carpet; repair existing walls for wallpaper
Bedroom (north)	repair existing	repair existing	new plaster	8'6"	remove existing wainscoting & patch plaster
Study	new strip oak	repair existing	new plaster	8'6"	strip oak laid east-west
Passage	carpet	new plaster	existing plaster	8'6"	repair existing floor for carpet
Bathrooms	ceramic tile	ceramic tile & plaster	new plaster	8'0"	ceramic tile around tub to ceiling
Bedroom (south)	repair existing	new & existing plaster	new plaster	8'6"	remove mantel & patch plaster
Dining room	new strip oak	new & existing plaster	existing plaster	11'0"	strip oak laid east-west
Kitchen	vinyl tile	east wall exposed brick	new plaster	10'0"	drop soffit* to 9' at east wall
Living room	repair existing	new & existing plaster	existing plaster	11'0"	patch & repair existing parquet floor & wood paneling

*A soffit is a built-out section of wall or ceiling, usually made to conceal pipes or ducts.

224

in relation to the way they fit into the floor plan. If there is any doubt about the clarity of necessary information, a detail drawing is in order.

• SPECIFICATIONS

Floor plans and detail drawings alone are not adequate to describe every aspect of the work to be done; a certain amount of written description is necessary to supplement the floor plans. This written material is called *specifications (specs)*. Specifications describe the work to be done, the methods of construction, the standards of workmanship, the manner of conducting the work, and the quality of materials and equipment to be used. Floor plans, detail drawings, and specs together are called *construction documents*. The construction documents enable contractors to bid construction costs accurately so that the owner can have a fixed price for the job. Ideally, a qualified contractor can build from the information given in the construction documents with no questions as to dimensions, materials used, or the slightest detail in construction.

Specifications should include all pertinent information and instructions in the following categories:

1. Demolition
2. Rough carpentry
3. Masonry
4. Plumbing
5. Wiring
6. Heating and air conditioning
7. Mechanical ventilation
8. Roofing
9. Plastering (or sheetrock)
10. Finish carpentry
11. Tile work
12. Ironwork
13. Cabinets, appliances, and other equipment

14. Hardware
15. Flooring
16. Painting

Following is a sample from actual specifications for a renovation so that you can see the kind of information given:

Bathroom and toilets shall have vitreous ceramic tile "Mosaic" pattern #200 cinnamon set in cement over M.L. and waterproof membrane or laid in waterproof mastic over ¾" waterproof plywood. Bathrooms shall have ceramic tile wainscot of selected color 48" high and to ceiling around tubs, glazed trim at all edges. Wall tile around tub shall be set in waterproof adhesive over cement plaster or set in wet cement. Supply recessed vitreous china accessory sets to match tile in baths.

Since the specifications are the instructions given to the contractor about what is expected, they must include everything you have in mind. Many problems in construction develop because there are no specifications or because the specs are not detailed enough. Even the simplest renovation job needs specifications. Make sure that every detail is down on paper.

• DEMOLITION

Demolition specifications include everything that must be removed (walls, ceilings, floors, cabinets and appliances, and so on), including all rubbish and debris. Any items that must be removed but are to be reused must be clearly specified, along with instructions for special care of these and other items to remain.

• ROUGH CARPENTRY

In the building business there are two kinds of carpentry: rough carpentry and finish carpentry. Rough carpentry is the work not visible to the eye when the job is complete because it is hidden behind plaster or sheetrock. The materials used during this phase of the job affect the finished product. If inferior-grade lumber is used for studding, it will warp, causing plaster to crack or sheetrock to pull away from the studs. If partitions are framed with two-by-threes instead of two-by-fours, or if studs are placed too far apart, the new walls will not be sturdy.

Specify that all new partitions be plumb. It is absolutely amazing how many modern carpenters do not seem to know how to use a level. If you do not know how to use one, now is not too soon to learn. Get a level, and practice using it at home. You will probably be surprised to find how few level surfaces there are in your present residence. The level should be your constant companion once construction begins. Use it on all surfaces, and insist that the workmen use theirs. They may think you a pest and complain, but they will have a new respect for you when they know you understand their tools.

• MASONRY

The term *masonry* applies to all work in brick and stone. In renovation, it applies to both new construction and repair of existing conditions. If plaster is to be removed to expose a brick wall, this work would come under the heading of masonry, because not only must the plaster be removed, but the brick must be repaired, cleaned, and either sealed or painted. Any repair to foundations or exterior masonry surfaces must be detailed. You might even put any concrete work to be done under this heading.

• PLUMBING

Plumbing is not limited to soil, water, and vent lines. It includes any plumbing in connection with the heating system, sprinkler system, yard drains, outside faucets, connections to city water and sewer systems, and gas lines. It also includes plumbing fixtures and trim. Everything should be clearly specified, from pipe size and material (brass, copper, cast iron, plastic, and so on) to the kind of toilet seat you want. You must make perfectly clear what plumbing is to remain, what is to be repaired, and what is to be new. The fixtures and trim should be designated by manufacturer, style number, and color—that way there can be no mistake. A provision should be made for cut-off valves in each bath and kitchen so that if a repair must be made, only the area to be worked on will be deprived of water. There should be an access panel for the tub, if possible, so that repairs can be made without damaging walls or floors.

• WIRING

If a total rewiring job is to be done, there should be an electrical plan for the entire house, showing the location of every fixture, switch, and outlet, along with all other wiring requirements. In addition, the quantity of each of these items (such as twenty-five outlets, thirteen switches) should be listed in the specs. Wiring includes new electrical service (usually done by the electric company but arranged for by the electrician), meters, circuit-breaker boxes, wiring for thermostats, air conditioning, special appliances, intercom and door-buzzer systems, and the installation of lighting fixtures.

If lighting fixtures are to be supplied by the electrician, they must be selected in advance and specified by manufacturer, style number, and color. In the case of recessed fixtures, these must be specified because the carpenter will have to frame out the opening in which they are housed.

Planning for wiring is not an easy job, so take the time to do it properly. Then make sure that everything is down on paper.

- HEATING AND AIR CONDITIONING

Like all other categories, this one includes new installation as well as repair of the existing system. All required work must be put in writing.

If a new system is to be installed, you will have an expert design it for you, and he will write all necessary specifications. Be sure he includes all work done by the various trades, such as electricians, plumbers, and carpenters.

The specs for the upgrading or repair of an existing system are usually more difficult. You may want to include a catch-all phrase such as "repair of existing system and installation of all necessary controls to have the system operate properly and efficiently." Older furnaces often do not have controls (such as an automatic hot-water cut-off valve) that make them easier to operate. Remember radiators or ducts, and registers. Old radiator valves should be replaced during renovation to prevent leaking after the floors are finished; with forced-air systems, ducts should be cleaned and registers replaced if they do not work. These things, and any others, must be specified if you want them done.

- MECHANICAL VENTILATION

You must specify the ductwork needed and fan size, etc. (see page 200 for discussion).

- ROOFING

Roofing and flashing, leaders and gutters, and skylights and other protrusions in the roof are included under this category.

The roof must be made watertight so that no leaks ruin your renovation. In houses with flat-topped roofs it is generally a good idea to replace the roof, since the expense in relation to potential damage is minimal. (Do not forget roofs on extensions.) Pitched roofs are much more expensive to replace, and a careful inspection should be made to determine whether they must be repaired or replaced. Remove the old roof before installing a new one: though it costs more, you will have a far better job. Leaders and gutters must be repaired or replaced, and skylights repaired to prevent damage to the interior.

The roofing business is notorious for fly-by-night operations. The kind of roof you wish to have installed, the repairs you want made, along with the size and material for leaders and gutters, must be precisely specified to ensure that you get what you want. You should also receive a guarantee of the work.

- PLASTERING OR SHEETROCK

Which you use is a matter of choice—plastering is usually more expensive, but unless you literally gut the house, some plastering will be required, if only for repair of what exists. Think twice before removing plaster, because it is superior to sheetrock in insulation against heat, cold, and noise.

The job of new plasterwork is done in three stages: (1) lathing is applied to the studs; (2) brown mortar is applied to the lathing; and (3) white plaster is applied over the brown coat once it is thoroughly dry. The thickness of the white coat as well as whether you want smooth or textured plaster must be specified.

When using sheetrock, the thickness of the material and the way it is installed and finished is of utmost importance. Five-eighth-inch sheetrock is required by many building codes, but contractors may try to save money by using half-inch material. Waterproof sheetrock should be used in baths and around kitchen sinks. Use of sheetrock nails and corner beads, along with proper taping of seams and spackling of nail heads and sanding, are important for good results. You want smooth new walls, whether they be plaster or sheetrock.

Make sure that existing plaster is properly repaired and joints between old and new plaster smooth. Also, you want no holes or cracks around moldings, baseboards, lighting fixtures, electrical face plates, and so forth.

• FINISH CARPENTRY

This work is a bag of worms and a constant source of homeowner's headaches everywhere. Finish carpentry includes installing and repairing existing doors, windows, moldings, baseboards, cabinets, medicine chests, hardware, or any other built-in feature of the house that requires the use of hammer and nails. The list of the finish carpenter's responsibilities is endless. The problems he can cause are bad enough in new construction, but they are even worse in renovation, where old things must be repaired and new things matched to the old.

Each item to be repaired must be specified, as well as where the new is to match the old. Each door and window should be described by size and design, using manufacturer's style numbers where possible. The kind of moldings around windows and doors should be specified. You cannot afford to miss a single item, since omission will either bring added cost or the lack of the item in the finished house. Go over the plans with a fine-tooth comb when writing specs for finish carpentry. When you have an architect write the specs, peruse his work equally diligently to see that he has forgotten nothing and has made no mistakes—architects are subject to errors and omissions like the rest of us humans.

• TILE WORK

Tile work refers to ceramic tile; other types of tile come under flooring. All tile should be specified by manufacturer, style number, and color. In making your selection, try to select a tile readily available from local suppliers, or you may be in for problems.

Tile can be installed in two ways. The old method is called a mud job. In wall installations, wire lath is nailed to the wall. Wet cemet is applied to the lathing, and the tile is applied to the wet cement. When the cement dries, the wall is grouted. In laying tile floors, wire lath is nailed to the floor. A thick layer of dry cement is applied over the lathing and leveled. The tile is laid on the dry cement, with the whole floor wet down when the tile is complete. When the cement dries, the floor is grouted.

The newer method is called a glue job. In wall installations, tile is merely glued to the wall and grouted when the glue dries. In floor installation, the same process is used, but often a concrete floor is poured first, to which the tile is glued. The glue job is obviously less expensive than the mud job.

Specs for tile work should include the method of installation, the color of grout to be used (gray, white, or white tinted to a specified color), the tile base around floors when there is no wall tile above, ceramic accessories (such as soap dishes, toilet paper holders, towel bars) if they are to be used, and details for custom-made shower stalls, tile counter tops, and so on.

· IRONWORK

Ironwork includes railings, burglar bars, fire escapes, metal stairs, and any repairs requiring welding. If you have a high stoop with a metal gate underneath, you may need an iron man to help with the installation of a new lock. Any ironwork, whether new work or repair, should be specified. Any new work, such as railings or stairs, should have a detail drawing. Ironwork can be expensive, so remember this when planning your renovation.

• CABINETS AND APPLIANCES

All appliances should be designated by brand name, model number, and color. They should be carefully chosen to make sure they will fit and function properly in the space designed for them.

Stock kitchen cabinets should be specified by manufacturer, style name, and finish, and each cabinet should be designated by size and number. A detailed plan of their location should be drawn so there can be no confusion.

If you are using custom-made cabinets, plans for them will have to be drawn by you, your architect, or the cabinetmaker and should include the materials to be used, the hardware, and the finish.

Specifications must also include information about counter tops.

• HARDWARE

Hardware includes a multitude of items: doorknobs, locks and latches, hinges, magnetic catches, door closers, sliding-door tracks, towel bars and other bathroom accessories when not ceramic, and so forth. Do not leave their selection to the contractor. Specify each item by manufacturer and style number, and be sure that selections are available locally if they are to be supplied by the contractor.

• FLOORING

It must be made clear whether existing floors are to be retained; if so, specifications should be given for their repair and finishing. Details about all new flooring should be given: grade and width for straight oak flooring; manufacturer and style number for parquet, vinyl, vinyl asbestos, and other tile and linoleum; and grade, color, and thickness for slate and marble. Methods of installation and finishes required should be specified.

- PAINTING

Painting refers to both interior and exterior work, and in the latter case includes steam cleaning as well as painting. Sandblasting, an alternative to steam cleaning, should *never* be used on exteriors, because it destroys the finish on brick and stone.

Preparation for painting in renovation work is almost more important than the painting itself. Painting will truly hide a multitude of sins, but it also points up flaws if proper preparation is not done. All nails and old wires should be removed, and cracks and holes filled with spackle and sanded smooth. Cracked or peeling paint should be scraped and sanded. Windows should be caulked and puttied inside and outside.

The brand name as well as the type (oil base or water base; flat, semigloss, or high gloss) and color of paint should be specified, along with the number of coats to be applied. Include also finishes for surfaces not to be painted. (See page 287–91 for tips on painting.)

- OTHER ITEMS

Specifications should also include all of the responsibilities of the contractor pertaining to permits, city inspections, and city approvals. There may be other items that do not fall under any of the aforementioned categories. Do not omit anything from the specifications. The purpose of specs is to describe, completely and accurately, the work to be done so that there can be no misunderstanding with contractor and workmen. It is your responsibility to make sure that plans and specs fulfill this requirement, no matter who prepares them. And some kind of specifications are needed for every job, no matter how small.

• DO YOU NEED AN ARCHITECT?

It is an architect's job to prepare construction documents (floor plans, detail drawings, and specifications), and if city approval of plans is required, the architect should obtain it. However, if you do not hire an architect, you must do this work yourself. If you are lucky enough to find a *highly* competent and reliable contractor and your renovation is a relatively simple job, he may be able to perform these services for you.

If there will be no wall changes, you may not need a complete set of floor plans, but if the arrangement of kitchen or bathroom interiors is to be changed, there should be plans for these rooms. If you plan to get cabinets and appliances from a kitchen planning center or home improvement contractor, they can draw plans for you as part of their service.

You should understand all of the services an architect performs so that you can decide whether you need him or not.

An architect can be hired to do anything from a simple set of floor plans to handling the complete renovation job from planning through construction. How much work you require of him will depend on your budget and the complexity of the renovation. The complete basic services of an architect include:

1. Design development
2. Construction documents
3. Bidding
4. Administration of the construction contract

Design development includes conferences with you to discuss what you need and want in your house, followed by sketches of ways to handle the space. These sketches are discussed, and a conclusion is reached on the plan that works best for you.

Then work is begun on the construction documents. When floor plans and specifications are in order, the plans are submitted to the city for necessary approval. When the plans have been approved, the architect will assist with the bidding, giving advice on the qualifications of prospective bidders and assistance in obtaining bids and awarding the construction contract.

During the construction, the architect will provide general administration of the construction contract, including periodic visits to the job to review the progress and quality of the work and to determine if the work is proceeding in accordance with the construction documents and contract. He will check on the contractor's applications for payment, determining the amounts due the contractor and issuing certificates for payment in such amount. If there are any changes to be made, he will prepare change orders asked for and approved by the owner. He will determine the date of substantial completion, turn over to the owner written guarantees provided by the contractor, and issue the final certificate for payment. At this point the renovation is complete, and the job of the architect is finished.

When hiring an architect, you normally sign a contract with him, setting forth the services he will perform and the amount of his fee. If you are contracting for all of the basic services just mentioned, the fee is generally based on a percentage of the construction cost, usually somewhere between 8% and 15% (but it can go as high as 20%). A schedule of payments to the architect will be set down in the contract, and usually is as follows:

An initial payment of 5% of the estimated cost, then:

Design development phase	35%
Construction documents phase	75%
Bidding phase	80%
Construction phase	100%

If you do not choose to use an architect for all of these basic services, you can contract for any one of several of them and negotiate a fee for the services to be performed. If you should decide not to use an architect at all, you must be prepared to perform all of his functions yourself.

Many cities require that plans be drawn by an architect (or licensed professional engineer). If this is the case in your city, you will have to hire an architect, if only to draw your plans. However, if the floor plan of your house is to be drastically changed, you will need the help of someone trained in design and familiar with local building codes and practices. No one quite fills the bill like an architect.

The complexity of building code regulations is one of the best reasons for hiring an architect. If he is experienced in renovation, he will be familiar with those aspects of the code dealing with alterations—which must be rigidly followed and which can be bent to solve a particular problem. A licensed architect not only has to pass a very difficult examination proving his knowledge of design, structure, mechanical and electrical engineering, heating, air conditioning, ventilation, and plumbing, but has also served an apprenticeship under a licensed architect. He may not have all the answers to your problems, but he is certainly far better equipped to handle them than you are.

- Selecting an Architect

The selection of an architect should not be taken lightly. You should not hire your best friend's brother or a social acquaintance unless he is truly qualified for your job. As with other professional services, it is often better to hire a total stranger with whom you have a purely business relationship than to have problems with hurt feelings when you treat a friend in a businesslike manner.

To quote from the American Institute of Architects' "Statement of Professional Services":

The selection of an architect is one of the most important decisions an owner makes when he undertakes a building program. In that decision, he selects a professional who is both a designer and an advisor who can translate his requirements into reality.

In hiring an architect, you are looking for a person who has the following qualifications:

1. He is experienced in renovation projects in your city.
2. His tastes are similar to yours.
3. He is willing and able to work within your budget.
4. He is enthusiastic about your project.
5. He has developed good working relationships with reputable contractors.
6. He continues to have good relationships with previous clients.

If you are only having the architect draw floor plans, all except number five are still important.

It is generally best to talk to several architects before making a selection. You will have some basis for comparison and the opportunity to get several points of view about your renovation. When interviewing an architect, you should talk to him about the services he can provide, what services he feels you need, his fee for those services, and whether he thinks your job can be done on your budget.

The selection of an architect should not be made on the basis of this interview alone. You should see some of his work and talk to the owners before making the decision to hire him. You are not interested in seeing the lovely office building he designed, because it is in no way relevant to what you are asking him to do. New construction and renovation are entirely different problems, and the architect right for one is not necessarily the choice for the other.

Here is what you should ask about any of the houses you see:

1. When was the renovation completed?
2. How long did it take from the time planning began?
3. How much did it cost?
4. Was there a budget for the job, and was it adhered to? If not, why?
5. Was the architect receptive to the owner's ideas and suggestions?
6. Who selected the contractor?
7. Were there problems during construction? If so, what kind?
8. Was the basic design of the house the owner's or the architect's?

All of these questions should be asked of both architect and owner, and their answers compared. In addition, you should ask the owner if he is happy with his house and if he would use the same architect again.

When looking at the houses, pay careful attention to the design. If an architect shows you only contemporary houses and you want a traditional house, he may not be the right architect for you. If you are planning to salvage much of the existing house and all the houses you are shown have obviously been gutted, beware. If you want an authentic restoration, ask your local preservation organization for a list of recommended architects. If an architect shows you only very expensive renovations and your budget is quite small, ask to see less expensive renovations he has done. If an architect shows you houses completed several years before, ask about his recent work.

Check the workmanship if the architect was responsible for assisting in the selection of the contractor and in administering the construction contract. If he was not involved in these phases, the responsibility for the workmanship lies purely with the owner. If you are planning to use an architect only to draw plans, the workmanship is less important. However, it would be a good idea to get the names of contractors on each job you see and make notes on the quality of the work they did. This list could be a good source when you are ready to get bids for your job.

The fee an architect charges will obviously be important, but the quality of the work you will receive from him is equally important. If you select an architect whose fee is lower but whose plans are bid far beyond your budget, you will have made a costly mistake. It would be far better to pay more to an architect who designs a house you can afford to build. You will live with and pay for the results of an architect's work for a long time, so you cannot take his selection lightly.

• WORKING WITH AN ARCHITECT

Hiring an architect does not mean you can turn everything over to him and forget about it. To quote once more from the AIA's "Statement of Professional Services":

It should be noted that the architect does not "supervise" the work, but based on his on-site observations as an architect he endeavors to guard the owner against defects and deficiencies in the work of the contractor. The contractor, and not the architect, is solely responsible for construction means, methods, techniques, sequences and procedures, and for safety precautions and programs in connection with the work. The architect likewise is not responsible for the contractor's failure to carry out the work in accordance with the contract documents.

Understanding this, it behooves you to keep abreast of the work being done on your house and not rely solely on the architect to see that it is done properly.

Give an architect all necessary information before hiring him—the size of your budget, what kind of house you want and why, and any special features of the house you wish to retain. He needs to know as much about you as possible if he is to design a house to fit your requirements. Once you hire him, do not let him force his ideas on you if you do not like them or cannot afford them.

You must never lose sight of the budget you have set for yourself. Too many extra ten-to-fifty-dollar items can shoot your budget in a hurry. If an architect has a weak point, it is usually in matters of economics. This is why you should check his ability to stay within a budget. You must continue to ask the cost of everything you wish to add and never let the architect lose sight of your budget; if you have no regard for it, you cannot expect him to be concerned about it. You might be wise to include in your contract with the architect a clause stipulating that he must redraw the plans at no additional cost if bids for the work exceed a specified amount. You must be prepared to lose time if you invoke this clause; therefore, it is better to make sure that you hire a budget-conscious architect in the first place.

To quote from an interview with Pietro Belluschi, M.I.T. dean of architecture and planning, that appeared in *House & Garden* under the title "Why Hire an Architect":

Some architects can't help seeing their work as monuments to themselves. If yours seems more interested in monumental achievements than in translating your wishes into the environment you expect, you have the wrong man. The main cause of conflict, however, is not design vs. practicality but rather cost vs. financial ability. Almost every client wants more house than he is willing or able to pay for. Architects know this perfectly well, but too few have the courage to get tough about keeping the budget down. Their failure to build houses for a promised amount of money has given the architectural profession its greatest black eye.

An architect uses very detailed plans and specifications, because the amount of time he can afford to spend on the job is limited. Most architects plan to make a specified number of inspections of the job and may charge for additional ones if they are required. In addition, the architect's fee does not include the cost of printing plans. Printing is not expensive, but if many sets of plans are needed, the bill can mount.

Architects often do not specify flooring, cabinets and appliances, lighting fixtures, and hardware when getting bids, but specify fixed dollar allowances instead. This method of bidding gives the owner more flexibility in his choices, but the owner must make certain that the allowances set are adequate to supply what is needed.

If the architect is administering the construction contract, it is best to let him select the contractor (after you have thoroughly checked the contractor yourself), because the relationship between architect and contractor is all-important—there are bound to be problems when these two men do not get along well.

Remember that you are dealing with a professional whose time is limited. If you are unable to make a decision, constantly change your mind, or do not know what you want, the architect will lose interest in your job.

• TERMINATING ARCHITECTURAL SERVICES

Changing architects is both expensive and time-consuming. You want to avoid it whenever possible by proper selection in the first place. However, there are times when you find you have made a mistake. It is better to terminate the services of an architect than to continue with the wrong one. You will owe the architect money for the work he has done for you up to the time of termination even though the work may be worthless to you. This is usually a bitter pill to swallow, but it can be less expensive than continuing with the same man.

12 How the Work Will Be Done

THERE IS MORE than one way to get the renovation done. You can hire a general contractor to handle the entire renovation; hire several contractors, each of whom is responsible for parts of the renovation (subcontract the job); or hire individual workmen on an hourly, daily, or weekly basis. An occasional renovator who is a real glutton for punishment has done the entire renovation himself— though this is impractical and in some cases illegal. Many a renovation job has been a combination of two or more of the above methods.

The first thing to consider is time. If the house is vacant during construction, the faster the job is completed, the sooner you can utilize the house you are paying for. If, however, the house is in acceptable condition, you may want to move right in and do the renovation over an extended period of time so that you can pay for it gradually. In either case, you should get any rental units finished as quickly as possible so that income can be realized.

A renovation done over several years usually means subcontracting the job, since the work will be done in a piece-meal fashion. However, if time is important, a general contractor is usually the answer.

• WHY HIRE A GENERAL CONTRACTOR?

Hiring a general contractor (G.C.) has many advantages. One man is responsible for all phases of the job from start to finish. He supplies the labor and material, along with scheduling and co-ordinating the work of the various trades. He may hire subcontractors to do all or parts of the job, or he may have a full crew of men working directly for him.

In building, there is much overlapping of trades. Take the simple matter of a recessed lighting fixture. The carpenter must frame out the opening in which the fixture is placed, but the electrician must supply the wiring and install the fixture. A mess is inevitably made in the process, and neither electrician nor carpenter feels he has any responsibility to clean it up—that job requires a laborer, not a skilled craftsman. The general contractor supplies the laborer as well as making sure that the carpenter is present when the electrician needs him and vice versa.

Situations like this are repeated and compounded throughout a renovation. Scheduling (having men and materials on the job when needed) is vital and is basically the reason for the existence of the general contractor. For this, plus his knowledge and experience (something a renovator usually does not possess), you pay him a fee. Why pay a G.C. when you can subcontract the job and save his fee? is a question often asked by renovators. Here is a list of reasons:

1. He supplies and schedules all labor, guaranteeing that work will be done according to specification. He has more leverage than you do in hiring and getting a good job from workmen and subcontractors because of potential future employment.

2. He supplies all material (which he is able to get at a better price) and sees that it is on hand when needed.
3. He pays all bills, relieving you of all bookkeeping chores: You pay only once. He also pays all workmen's insurance and benefits.
4. He gets all permits and copes with city inspectors.

• SUBCONTRACTING THE JOB YOURSELF

There are many renovators who have subcontracted their own work quite successfully. The simpler the renovation plan, the easier it is to subcontract the job yourself. The more complex the job, the greater the need for a competent G.C.

There are two conditions under which subcontracting your own job is virtually mandatory: (1) if the job is to be done gradually over an extended period of time; (2) if the entire job is so small that no G.C. would be interested in it.

It is seldom advisable or even feasible to do your own subcontracting unless you are living in the house or can be on the job several hours every day. There is a constant need for co-ordination and supervision (what happens when the carpenter has not appeared and the electrician is waiting for him?). If you cannot be there, you should hire someone to be responsible as foreman—usually the head carpenter.

The only practical way of subcontracting is to hire subcontractors who will be responsible for each part of the work, supplying all labor and materials needed. Each subcontractor would have his own contract, his own set of construction documents, and would be responsible for city inspections of his part of the job and for insurance and benefits for his workmen. In short, he would be acting as a G.C. for a portion of the job. If you should have to supply materials, you would be involved in ordering and scheduling deliveries, credit with suppliers, record keeping, and many frustrations.

- HIRING INDIVIDUAL WORKMEN

Another way of getting the job done is to hire individual workmen instead of subcontractors. This usually involves supplying materials yourself and paying wages, including social security, workmen's compensation, unemployment insurance, and so on. You would also have to keep an elaborate set of books and, in essence, set up your own contracting firm. An occasional day laborer to help to do odd jobs is fine, but a steady crew of employees is not recommended.

The Stanforths were unintentionally dragged into such a situation when their contractor walked out and left them with a crew of unpaid workmen. They had a hard enough time meeting payrolls and were unaware of required workmen's benefits. When the job was finished, one workman applied for unemployment compensation. Neither the Stanforths nor the contractor had paid for unemployment insurance. Although innocent victims of a dishonest contractor, the Stanforths nonetheless were hounded by the New York State Department of Labor until they made a settlement (though the contractor got off without paying because he could not be found).

To avoid having this happen to you, hire workmen by the job, as contractors, so that *they* are responsible for workmen's benefits.

Will you actually save money by taking on the job of contracting yourself? Maybe yes, maybe no. Many people who feel they save money by contracting the job themselves fail to consider the time element, which in some cases can have dollar value. When a house is vacant during renovation, time is money. If it will take you a year to subcontract the job yourself when a G.C. could do it in six months, you must add the cost of paying for your current residence for an additional six months to the cost of the renovation. If you are paying three hundred and fifty dollars a month rent, using a G.C. would save you twenty-one hundred dollars.

Philadelphia architect Benjamin Kitchen did his own house, working evenings and weekends. It took him three years. When he finished, he realized that he would have been better off financially if he had saved for three years and hired a general contractor to do the work.

· DOING YOUR OWN WORK

Most renovators have a bit of do-it-yourself in them, and hardly one has failed to handle a hammer or paintbrush at some point during the renovation. People who had previously been all thumbs have learned to build cabinets and lay floors. Few, however, have been able to do all the work themselves.

Be realistic about what you can reasonably accomplish. Taking on more than you can do comfortably only leads to frustration. A renovation should be stimulating, not a drag. Select those jobs that you can do and still have time to talk to your wife (husband) or read to the children. Do-it-yourself projects are fun and rewarding when taken in palatable doses, but like too much liquor for too many days in a row, too many projects can give you a never-ending hangover.

Usually it is the finishing details that can be most practically and effectively done by the owner: special cabinet-work, flooring, painting, or wood stripping. Whatever you choose to do yourself, remember that it must be co-ordinated with the rest of the work so that you do not hold up construction if your job is not completed on schedule. Since someone will have to pay the men who are losing time, it may cost you more than you can save.

- WHICH METHOD WORKS BEST FOR YOU?

Hiring a general contractor does not mean that he must do all the work on the house or that the entire renovation must be completed while he is working. You can hire a G.C. to do all the basic work, saving most of the finishing details to complete at your leisure.

Martha Stamm has often used a general contractor to avoid scheduling or dealing with building inspectors. However, she usually hires subcontractors for floor finishing, painting, and custom cabinet work, and she supplies such items as appliances, lighting fixtures, and decorative hardware.

The method you choose may be one or a combination of several. But regardless of which you use, you must plan for how the work will be done and who will be responsible for each task. The owner is the manager of his house. Even though he may do some or all of the work himself, he must have a clear picture of the project from start to finish, from purchase through planning and construction, if the renovation is to go smoothly and be completed to his satisfaction.

- OBTAINING BIDS FOR CONSTRUCTION

Before the construction documents are sent to contractors for bids, any necessary city approvals should be obtained. Sometimes plans must be amended in order to get city approval. If plans were sent out for bids prior to approval, amended plans would have to be resubmitted to all bidders.

The construction documents must be designed in accordance with the way the work is to be done. If you plan to do some of the work yourself or if you are subcontracting the job, the specifications must clearly state the responsibility of each party involved.

You should get more than one bid for the job (or for each phase in the case of subcontracting), so that you can get the best price possible. But getting bids is not a case of the more the merrier; the contractor must have assurance that he has a chance of getting the job if his price is right. Three bidders is the standard number.

A complete set of construction documents is sent to each bidder; all must have the same information if the bids are to be properly assessed. Remember, it takes time for contractors to make their estimates. You seldom receive a bid for a week after the construction documents are distributed, and two to four weeks is normally required.

Finding reputable contractors to bid on the work is not always easy. If you are using an architect, he is the logical source for competent contractors. Your local lumber dealer and plumbing supply house are good potential sources for names of reliable contractors, and your city or state preservation office may keep a list of contractors and craftsmen sensitive to restoration. Renovators tend to band together into organizations, and these, along with individual renovators, can often provide information on contractors. Real estate brokers are another potential source of names. And if you saw houses in checking on architects and followed the suggestion to take the names of contractors, by all means use those whose work you have already seen. Friends, relatives, the building department, your local AIA chapter, even the Yellow Pages of the phone book are potential sources. But do some checking on a contractor before allowing him to bid.

· METHODS OF BIDDING

There are two methods of bidding: (1) *fixed price* and (2) *cost plus.* The method used depends on the individual contractor and the area in which you live. Fixed-price bidding is the most common, but because of the unforeseen difficulties involved in renovation, many contractors will not bid a fixed price.

A *fixed-price* bid means that the contractor has carefully studied the construction documents, estimated the cost to do the work, added his profit, and come up with a cost for the job to be done. Once the contract is signed, the contractor is obligated to perform the work specified in the contract for the price agreed upon. However, any change made in the construction documents after the contract is signed gives the contractor an opportunity to alter his price.

In a *cost-plus* job, the contractor also estimates what he thinks the cost will be, but he does the job on the condition that you agree to meet all of his costs plus an agreed-upon fee for himself (usually a percentage of the cost of the job). On payday he submits bills for his expenses since the previous payday, and you pay him that amount. Cost-plus contracting is sometimes referred to as "time and materials."

Sometimes it is possible to include an *upset price* in a cost-plus contract. This means that a maximum price is guaranteed for the job as specified. If the contractor's cost is below the upset price, the owner receives the savings; but if the cost is higher, the owner will pay no more than the upset figure.

There are obvious risks in hiring a contractor on a cost-plus basis; there is no incentive for him to keep costs down. The cost-plus contractor must be impeccably honest and reliable, because he could easily pad his expenses. However, a fixed-price contract with a dishonest or insolvent contractor is worthless, so the question is not really so much one of bidding method as of the contractor's dependability.

• WHAT IF ALL THE BIDS ARE TOO HIGH?

This is indeed a sad day in the life of any renovator, and we wish we could report that it did not happen often.

If all bids are too high, either the plan for the renovation was too elaborate for your budget, or the contractors who bid were too expensive for your pocketbook.

There are many contractors whose cost for the same job may be miles apart. Just because a contractor is expensive does not mean that you will receive value for the dollar. Though you should always be wary of a bidder who is substantially below all others, an inexpensive price does not necessarily mean inferior work. There are factors other than labor and materials that may influence a contractor's bid. If he is very busy and does not need the work, he may bid higher than usual because the job would mean hiring additional men and more work for himself. On the other hand, a contractor may bid a job very close if he thinks it would bring repeat business or new customers. The same could be true if the job came at a slow time when it would mean the difference between keeping valuable men and laying them off.

The most obvious reason for the difference between bids is the overhead of the contractor and the wages he pays his employees. A contractor who hires union workmen is usually more expensive than one who uses non-union labor. If the contractor actually works on the job, as is the case with many small contractors, his price will usually be lower than that of purely administrative contractors.

Talk to the contractors who bid, and ask them why their bids were higher than the budget you set. They might be able to make suggestions for alterations in the plans that will lower the cost. One might even be able to suggest a contractor who could do the job within your budget.

Before drastically altering your plans, try to get bids from less expensive reputable contractors. But do not panic and accept a low bid without properly checking on the contractor.

If you are unable to find a reliable contractor at the right price and are unwilling or unable to pay the additional cost of renovation, you must redraw your plans on a more modest scale. In redrawing the plans, try to make provisions for those things which can be added later.

• SELECTING A CONTRACTOR

Before hiring a contractor, you must check him thoroughly. The importance of checking a contractor applies to subcontractors as well as general contractors. The building business has its share of incompetents and even outright crooks. You certainly do not want to entrust your hard-earned money to either.

The contractor, like the architect, will be with you for a long time, and you will either live happily or unhappily with the results of his labor. As the AIA Statement of Professional Services says, "the contractor is solely responsible for the construction," and you are solely responsible for whom you hire to do it.

You cannot depend on the law to protect you from a dishonest contractor. A construction contract is only worth as much as the man who signs it. You and your property are readily accessible to liens and lawsuits, whereas the contractor operating under a corporate name can liquidate his corporation or see that it has no assets.

A corporation can be formed by filing the necessary papers with the office of the Secretary of State. It is a simple matter and the cost is usually minimal. The corporate laws do not require corporations to have financial stability, but they do limit the liability of officers and stockholders. Most businesses that operate under corporate names are legitimate operations in business to provide goods and services to make an honest profit. However, the corporate structure is also a haven for con men.

If the contractor you hire operates under a corporate name, it is the corporation you must petition or sue for redress of grievances. The contractor himself may have assets, but if the corporation has none, it will do you no good to win a lawsuit. Therefore, you must make as certain as is humanly possible that the man and his corporation have a record of honest dealings, reputable work, and solvency. You cannot depend on trust or assumptions, and you cannot rely on someone else to check for you. (Do not assume that you should not check the contractor because your architect recommends him, even if they have worked together before. Your architect's apology is small consolation if the contractor goes bankrupt or walks out on your job.)

Take the time to do a thorough check. No matter how pressed for time you think you are, you can lose more time and a great deal of money if you are careless in this investigation.

The truly amazing fact that emerges is that countless bright, intelligent people have employed architects and contractors without any indication of their qualifications.

When a family decides to purchase a washing machine, they go to a number of stores, study consumer guides, question repairmen, ask friends whether they are satisfied with theirs. And yet when they are going to spend thousands of dollars on their homes, few make any inquiry at all about past performance of contractors before signing a construction contract. Small wonder that disreputable contractors find such easy prey. A plumber, electrician, or roofer should be investigated at least as carefully as a washing machine.

· How to Check on a Contractor

To avoid problems during construction, investigate any contractor before hiring him. Here is what you should check:

1. First, easiest, and most obvious—is he or his corporation listed in the telephone book? Does he have an office or merely an answering service or mail drop? Go and find out. (This is a good quick check on anyone who

wants to do work for you. Fly-by-night con men seldom have offices and listed phones.)

2. How long has he or his corporation been in business? (If it is a new business or new corporation, check the background of the owner. What did he do before and whom did he work for?)

3. Ask for a list of several of his suppliers, including major ones such as lumber and plumbing supply dealers, and find out whether his credit is good and over how long a period of time. (Beware of a contractor who cannot get credit.)

4. Ask where he has his bank account, and find out how long he has had the account, whether he maintains a substantial balance, whether his checks bounce, and whether he has loans he is repaying. (This, of course, applies to corporate accounts if that is his way of doing business.)

5. The most important means of checking (and not to be omitted) is references from people whose houses he has completed. You should have at least three (the more, the better), and at least one that is recent. Do not merely telephone (they could be friends or family). Interview the owner, and see the house the contractor worked on. Look at the workmanship (not the design): is it done well? How extensive was the job? Does it compare in size to yours? (If it was a minor job, do not accept it as a bona fide reference.) Ask the owner if he is satisfied with the quality of the work. Does everything function properly? Were there any problems during construction? What were they, and whose fault? Was the work done on schedule? (It almost never is, so a short time beyond the schedule is not enough for disqualification.) Does the contractor stand behind his work, returning to make corrections or repairs? Were there many extra charges? Why, and for what? Were there any liens?

6. Have a check made through your lawyer or the bank that holds your mortgage to find out if there is any

litigation pending against the contractor or his corporation.

We all look for bargains, particularly when dealing in thousands of dollars. But to do so can be a mistake. If a contractor is honest, he must make a reasonable profit in order to stay in business. He has to pay workmen and buy materials to produce a good job. As in any business, overhead and profit must be added to these costs. You cannot expect the contractor to cut the price below the level at which he can make a profit and still deliver a sound construction job. If you have reason to believe he is deliberately underbidding merely to get the job (without any reasonable explanation), beware.

This does not mean that some contractor's bids cannot be substantially lower than others; there can indeed be a very wide range of difference. But weigh all factors carefully, and make sure the lowest bidder has a solid reputation and record.

• THE CONSTRUCTION CONTRACT

Although many renovators have hired contractors with no agreement other than a verbal one, this is simply asking for trouble. Just as the contract for the purchase of property sets down the terms and conditions under which the property will be bought, the construction contract spells out the terms and conditions under which the renovation work will be done. Any agreement not incorporated in a contract is not binding on either side.

Lien laws protect the right of workmen (including contractors and architects) and suppliers to be paid for work and materials that go into property by enabling them to make claims (liens) against the property for unpaid bills. A proper construction contract is the owner's means of protecting himself against unjustified claims, because it specifies the work to be done, the price of the work, and the responsibilities of each party.

You should have a written agreement with anyone who is doing work on your house. How detailed this agreement should be will depend on the amount of work to be done. Any contract involving a large sum of money should be discussed with your lawyer, and it is best to have him read the agreement before you sign it. He may have some valuable suggestions to make, and he will certainly be able to tell if you are giving away your right arm without knowing it.

Any construction contract should contain the following:

1. Name and address of owner
2. Name and address of contractor
3. Address of property where work is to be done
4. Time of commencement and completion
5. List of construction documents (plans, specs, etc.) on which the work is based
6. The price of the work
7. A schedule of payment
8. Guarantee of the work
9. Proof of workmen's compensation insurance
10. Signature of both parties
11. No blank spaces that could be filled in later to the detriment of the owner

There should be two signed copies of the contract, one for the owner and one for the contractor.

The construction contract is the basis of any claims against the contractor, so it is important that the contract cover everything of interest to the owner. The AIA prints standard contracts that come with a set of general conditions stating the responsibilities of each party and procedures for terminating the contract. AIA document A-111 is used when the basis of payment is a stipulated sum (fixed price), and AIA document A-101 is used when the basis of payment is the cost of the work plus a fee (cost plus). These documents are available through an architect or from your local AIA office. If your construction contract is not an AIA one, it should still cover all items discussed in the AIA General Conditions.

Contracts are for the benefit of both contractor and owner, and your contractor should want one as much as you do. However, you should not wait for him to provide one but should discuss the contract when talking to him about the job. Construction contracts are standard procedure with architects who administer the construction phase and with most general contractors. However, subcontractors and independent craftsmen are often lackadaisical about written agreements. You cannot afford to be.

• Commencement and Completion

Setting a date for completion of work in the contract usually has little meaning unless there is a lawsuit. However, it is possible to include a penalty clause for work not completed on schedule. (This clause is obviously binding only if the owner makes no changes in the plans and specifications.) The penalty is usually expressed in a dollar amount to be subtracted from the price of the job for each day beyond the deadline that work is not complete. Contractors are generally reluctant to agree to such a penalty in renovation work because so much is unknown until work actually begins. Often the contractor will agree to the penalty clause only if he receives a bonus for finishing ahead of schedule.

• LIST OF CONSTRUCTION DOCUMENTS

The plans and specifications must be a part of any construction contract. These documents should be listed in the contract as follows:

    _____ pages of floor plans

    _____ pages of electrical plans

    _____ pages of specifications

    _____ pages of detail drawings

To make certain that there is no misunderstanding about what is in each of these documents, the owner should have one complete set with each page initialed by both himself and the contractor.

• THE PRICE OF THE WORK

The price quoted in the contract is based on the work described in the construction documents. If work is not specified in the contract or if changes are made in the work specified, the contractor has the right to additional money. The construction contract should make provision for changes or additions to the work. (The AIA General Conditions make such provision.)

• SCHEDULE OF PAYMENT

Every job, no matter how small, should have an agreement on when and how payments are to be made. The payment schedule should be fair to both parties—the contractor should not be paid too much in advance, and the owner should not expect the contractor to finance the renovation.

Payments are normally made in stages as work progresses. If a construction loan is financing the work, payments to the contractor must be co-ordinated with the bank's takedown schedule, so that the owner is not obligated to pay out money he does not yet have.

The contract should specify that the contractor obtain any necessary approvals and certificates from the city and turn over to the owner all warranties for equipment before the final payment is made. The usual procedure is to hold ten percent of the price until the job is completed, but the larger the final payment, the more leverage the owner has in getting the job completed to his satisfaction.

- GUARANTEES

All work should be guaranteed, and the terms of such guarantees spelled out in the contract. When dealing with a general contractor, you should have guarantees on the work of all subcontractors as well as a general guarantee from the G.C. A time limit should be specified for repair of any problem covered by the guarantees.

- WORKMEN'S COMPENSATION INSURANCE

You, as the owner, are responsible for injury to anyone on your property. To protect yourself against claims for injury, you carry liability insurance. However, liability insurance covers normal conditions and may not cover injury during construction. In such a situation a serious injury could wipe you out financially.

Special insurance (workmen's compensation) is available to cover injury to men on construction jobs. Most states require contractors to carry this insurance for their employees. However, you must be sure that any contractor you hire has a workmen's compensation insurance policy in effect. If there are men working on your house who are not so covered, you should take out a workmen's compensation policy yourself.

Every construction contract should contain any agreement made between you and the contractor. The more detailed the contract, the better protected you are in case of difficulty. However, no contract can protect you against problems with a dishonest contractor. The contract sets down rights and responsibilities, but enforcing the terms of the contract is another matter. The only protection you have against a disreputable contractor is not hiring him.

• PERFORMANCE BONDS

A *performance bond* is an insurance policy guaranteeing that work will be completed as specified in the construction contract. The bond is obtained and paid for by the contractor, but the cost is included in the price of the work. The bond is provided by a surety company (bonding company), which must be satisfied that the contractor is experienced and financially sound enough to perform the work for the agreed price.

Usually only major construction jobs are so insured, because few small contractors are able to meet the requirements of the bonding companies and because the companies themselves do not find it worthwhile to check out contractors' qualifications for a small job. However, some FHA insured mortgages require a performance bond or other guarantee of completion.

A contractor who is "bondable" may refer to himself as a bonded contractor, though this only means that he is able to get a performance bond. If the owner wishes to have this insurance, he must so request and stipulate in the specifications. The bond itself should be incorporated in the construction contract.

Though a performance bond may appear to be the answer to all renovation problems, it has its drawbacks. Although the surety company is obligated to pay for completion of the work if the contractor should default on the contract, legal complications can cause lengthy delays, and the quality of the work may not necessarily conform to the owner's expectations. The cost of a performance bond is relatively small, provides protection against liens, and is worth the investment when it is available. However, it is no substitute for careful checking on the contractor and proper supervision of the job.

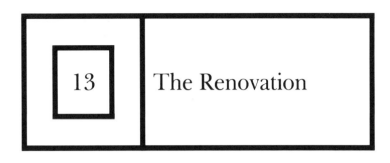

| 13 | The Renovation |

THE DAY THAT WORK finally begins is a milestone, one you thought would never come if you did proper planning in advance. If you have followed the recommended procedures and precautions, there should be no major problems from this point on. (If there are, you should be equipped to handle them.) This is not to say that you can go on vacation and return to the finished house. There are always problems in renovation, because you never are sure what you will find once you start tearing down walls. But the problems can be solved readily *if* you keep track of the job and have a good relationship with the contractor and workmen. You must use good common sense, being reasonable at all times without letting the contractor take advantage of you.

- HOW WORK PROGRESSES

You should understand the various stages of construction and the plans and specifications for your job in order to know whether work is progressing as it should. There are no hard and fast rules in renovation construction because at least some of the existing features of the house will remain. However, a logical order must be followed if work is to progress smoothly and rapidly; if new partitions are closed up before wiring, etc., is put in, you will have real problems.

Construction work falls into two general classifications: the rough and the finish. The *rough* encompasses everything hidden inside the walls and includes studs (the wooden framework that supports the walls), wiring, pipes, ducts, and flues. The *finish* begins with enclosing the walls and includes all work that must be done to finish the job.

Renovation work often begins at the top of the house and progresses downward (except for rough plumbing, where pipes must be installed from bottom to top). The reason for this is logical: workmen carry their tools to the top, finish the work there, and move down to the next floor, so that when the top floor is complete it can be sealed off and not disturbed while work goes on below. (Were the process reversed, work completed could be damaged by workmen going through to get upstairs.) In a four- or five-story house, it is not unusual to find work at a different stage on each floor.

If work is being contracted by trades, each trade will want to finish its phase of the work at one time. A plasterer generally will not come to plaster only one floor at a time when there are several floors to be plastered; he wants to bring his men and materials to finish the job in one trip. However, when a contractor has men working directly for him, he has more flexibility in scheduling the trades and generally has workmen who are skilled in more than one trade. Therefore, the work of the various trades can progress at a different pace than when the trades are subcontractors; one floor can be almost complete with very little work having been done on another floor.

As soon as demolition is complete, the carpenter can

begin laying out the new floor plan. (If the house is to get all new wiring, the electrician must provide temporary lines until the new electrical system is complete and usable.) As soon as all partitions are in place, the plumber and electrician can begin their work. Before partitions can be enclosed, all structural work, piping (for plumbing and heating), wiring (including prewiring for phones and cable T.V.), duct work (for heating, air conditioning, mechanical ventilation, and venting for dryers and stove hoods), flue work (for furnace and fireplaces), and insulation must be done. Changes or additions to the rough after the finish has begun require tearing walls open.

Before the finish is begun, the house should be sealed to prevent damage. This includes roofing and flashing, gutters and leaders, new windows and repair to existing ones, the closing of any holes or openings in the exterior, masonry repair to exterior walls, and any necessary waterproofing of the exterior. Exterior painting can be done then or later, but if masonry repair requires the use of scaffolding, it is best to have painting done at the same time.

The finish begins with enclosing new walls and patching of existing ones, and includes all items visible to the eye. The plumber and electrician will return to finish their work, other craftsmen will appear on the scene, and the carpenter(s) will be ever present.

How work will progress once walls are closed will vary, but certain work must be done first. Door jambs must be installed before moldings. New flooring goes in before baseboards. Doors are hung at the very end of the job so they will not get banged up or in the workmen's way.

In bathrooms, tubs are installed as part of the rough, because they must be in place before walls can be closed. Floor and wall tile are installed before the remaining fixtures are put in.

In kitchens, built-in sinks and appliances cannot be installed until cabinets and counter tops are in place. New flooring is put down before removable appliances are moved in.

Unfinished wooden floors can be laid early in the finish but prefinished wood flooring and ·tile (except in baths) should go in just before painting to prevent scratching and other damage.

The finish includes not only all new work but also the repair of existing features. All finish work, except floor finishing and installation of decorative equipment such as lighting fixtures, should be complete before painting is done if the paint job is to stay fresh and clean. The last item in renovation should be the sanding and finishing of wood floors. When the floor finisher departs, the renovation should be complete.

The finish will move rapidly at first and then slow down to a snail's pace toward the end. It is here that constant checking is mandatory to be certain that plans and specifications are being followed and that the quality of workmanship is acceptable. The rough might be considered the technical phase of renovation, where the basic elements for convenience and comfort are laid out; the finish, the aesthetic phase, where flaws that may frustrate you later become manifest.

• POSSIBLE PROBLEMS

Because renovation is a combination of existing conditions and new construction, it holds a degree of uncertainty that is not present in building a house from scratch. No matter how much planning has been done in advance, unexpected problems can arise. Plumbing that you thought could remain may suddenly spring a leak. A demolished partition may reveal a pair of old doors that you would like to use. When old plumbing fixtures are removed, you may find the beams beneath them notched and rotting. Beams may be located where ducts or pipes are to run.

As the owner of an old house, you must be prepared to be flexible should unforeseen trouble arise. A wall may have to be shifted slightly, causing some problems with the floor plan. There may be extra charges for replacing beams or repairing a ceiling that suddenly gives way.

As there are no hard and fast rules for how the work progresses, there are no pat solutions for handling problems that occur during renovation. You must just use good common sense, be prepared to compromise a little, and always keep your sense of humor. You too will find those trying times can make humorous anecdotes at cocktail parties in the future.

The problems that are difficult to cope with are caused by the following:

1. Inadequate construction documents
2. Lack of a proper construction contract
3. Failure to check the contractor before hiring him
4. Lack of communication between owner, architect, and contractor
5. Changes made after construction begins
6. Paying the contractor too much in advance
7. Contractor having underbid the job
8. Lack of skilled workmen and sloppy workmanship
9. Improper supervision

Most of these problems can be avoided.

· ADDITIONAL CONSTRUCTION CHARGES ("EXTRAS")

Most extra charges during construction occur because of inadequate construction documents, an inadequate contract, or changes made after work has begun.

The plans and specifications are your instructions to the contractor and his workmen. The more detailed the construction documents, the fewer problems that arise and the less supervision the job requires. You cannot expect the contractor to read your mind. He will know what you want only if you have told him. The instructions that are enforceable are those included in the construction contract.

If proper planning has been done, you will have taken care of all your needs and drawn up exact plans and specs for the job. There may be slight changes or additions during construction—extra shelves in a closet, another light for the bedroom, and so on—but these should be minor. With adequate plans and specifications incorporated into a detailed construction contract, there can be no additional charges for the work covered therein. There may be extra costs for unforeseen problems such as replacing a rotten beam or a ceiling that falls through no fault of the contractor, but if you have a reputable contractor and have been fair and reasonable with him, these costs should be held to a minimum.

Any changes made after construction begins can be costly. If you discover a change that must be made, get a price in writing before you have the work done. If his costs are running higher than he expected, even the most honest contractor has a tendency to charge more than the work is truly worth when the price is set after the fact. Get the price for everything before authorizing additional work, and keep a running record for yourself so that you are aware of the total—those small charges can add up quickly.

Some changes can be made for little or no extra cost if they are made in time. The location of a closet or other partition can be changed slightly in advance of framing. It usually makes no difference to the contractor if a wall is moved a foot or so in either direction, provided the work does not entail the replacement of a floor or ceiling that was to be retained. If, however, a closet is to be enlarged, requiring additional labor and materials, you should expect to pay an additional price. If changes involve work that has already been done, the contractor will be frustrated, his men will complain, and he will probably make you pay through the nose for it.

The more familiar you are with the job being done and the progress being made, the easier it will be for you to discover the changes you may want to make in advance of construction in that area. If you are reasonable and use some common sense when making changes, extra expenses can be kept to a minimum.

• Working with the Contractor

By far the most serious problems that occur in construction are the result of the owner's failure to investigate the contractor before hiring him. The best contract and the most detailed plans and specifications are meaningless to a man who is unreliable.

The more you know about the man (men) you hire, the easier it will be to work with him. There is no such thing as a perfect contractor, because renovation work is difficult, particularly when there is much salvaging to be done, and the job of the contractor is a tedious and trying one. If you know that the man you are hiring has a tendency to be slow, you can begin prodding him to finish on schedule from the very beginning.

You must establish good communication with the contractor from the start. The contractor, not his men or subcontractors, is responsible for the job—you must tell *him* if something displeases you. How is the contractor to know if you are dissatisfied unless you say so?

You should meet regularly with the contractor to discuss the progress of work and any problems that have come up. (If your architect is administering the construction contract, he should deal with the contractor and you should meet with him regularly to direct all questions through him to the contractor. The contractor can have only one boss.

The relationship between architect, owner, and contractor should always be kept on a reasonable basis. Raised voices seldom accomplish anything but anger.

Money is the only real leverage you have. It is the anticipation of payment that provides the incentive for the contractor to move ahead with the job. Do not let your contractor lose his incentive. Draw up a fair payment schedule, and then stick to it.

A contractor will often ask for money in advance, but an owner is unwise if he gives in. Contractors who are doing more than one job at a time often feed money back and forth from one job to another. You want to make sure that your money is being used exclusively for your work. Once it goes into someone else's job, the contractor may find himself in trouble and request additional money. Giving in only allows him to go further into the hole. If your contractor is in financial difficulty, the sooner you know about it, the better. When most of the money has been paid for a job that is less than half finished, the owner is in trouble. Terminating a construction contract is not easy, but it is best done at the earliest possible moment to avoid large financial losses.

• SUPERVISION

The more you know about the work being done on your house, the sooner you can detect any serious problems. Even if you are paying an architect to administer the contract, and even though you trust and respect him, you should check the progress and quality of the work yourself as often as possible. It is *your* money that is being spent, *your* house that is being renovated, and no one will be as concerned as you. If something is not being done properly, the chances are fairly good that you will find out about it by being there and observing carefully, even though you think you know nothing about construction. If you are not using an architect, you would be wise to check the job every day.

Even with detailed plans and specs, someone must see that they are being followed. Contractors and workmen can be particularly independent about what they install, feeling that if they put it in, it has to stay whether the owner likes it or not.

Tile men are notorious; there are innumerable tales of owners who found different tile installed than what they had chosen, and submitted meekly to living with the tile man's choice rather than their own. However, one such autocrat met his match in Dorothy Friedman.

Experienced as a hard-working interior designer, Dorothy knows what she wants and insists upon getting it. What she wanted for her children's bathroom was yellow fixtures and matching tile. Awaking one morning in her suburban home, she had a presentiment that something was going wrong in the renovation of her Manhattan brownstone. Sure enough, when she arrived on the job there was a man standing in her yellow bathtub putting brown tiles on the wall. Dorothy's tirade of abuse produced the complacent assurance that the color was "fawn," not the four-letter word she called it, and that it was the very latest thing, the most popular shade. What's more, he refused to remove it. Satisfied that he had quelled the tempest, he was occupied in boasting to the contractor about his skill in handling homeowners when Dorothy returned with a screwdriver borrowed from the electrician. Stepping into the tub next to the workman, she began flicking off the offending tiles. As they fell shattering, the tile contractor lost his smugness."Stop," he pleaded, "before you break them all so I can't even return them!" Needless to add, the Friedmans have a yellow bathroom.

The Stanforths arrived too late to avoid one disaster, and almost too late to prevent another. The small front parlor of their house had ornamentation that had convinced them to buy the house. The foot-wide plaster frieze just below the ceiling had every wreath, garland, and crossed torch intact. In the flat part there was only one small hole, where a sprinkler pipe had run through. Dozens and dozens of times the contractor and men had been warned not to damage the frieze. And yet when the plasterer got up on a ladder to patch the three-inch hole, he stripped off three feet of the canvas-backed frieze and threw it on the floor! it took Deirdre Stanforth weeks of striving and two unsuccessful attempts to make a mold from the remaining frieze to recast and patch the needless destruction.

To complete their apparently willful destruction of this one perfect room, the contractor's men almost succeeded in throwing out the incredibly elaborate fireplace. They were busy plastering up the opening when Deirdre and the architect arrived one day for a routine inspection. Apparently ignoring the plans, the workmen were under the impression that this fireplace was to be eliminated. It very nearly was, because most of the parts were rescued at the door, where they were awaiting removal by the rubbish truck. Not all could be found. Several pieces were broken off and missing from the sculptured, green-patinaed bronze sidepieces, one of the three sections of iron backing (made with wreaths to match the frieze) was gone, and the pink marble facing was cracked in several places. It all had to be painstakingly pieced back together again.

Supervision is essential to avoid these and other catastrophes. Even the most reputable and honest of contractors can make mistakes. A dependable contractor will rectify them, but the time wasted and the nuisance of having workmen in the house after the job is supposed to be complete are annoying and sometimes costly. There are even times when it is impractical to rectify mistakes after they have been made.

Progress of work should be checked regularly and the house thoroughly inspected on each visit. You or the architect should be on hand when the new floor plan is being laid out so that any difficulties can be solved immediately.

Finishing details in a house are particularly important. The most common problems are the faulty installation of moldings around windows and doors, improper placement of light switches and outlets, doors that open the wrong way or are hung improperly, small items omitted (such as locks on windows), substitutions made for items specified, and generally sloppy workmanship. Poor workmanship is an all-too-common occurrence in renovation work as well as in new construction. The construction business often seems to train butchers rather than craftsmen. If poor workmanship is a problem in your renovation, discuss it with the contractor as soon as it first comes to your attention. Sometimes workmen are careless simply because they have not been properly trained. Getting to know the workmen and praising them when they do a good job can often work miracles. Many times workmen do not understand how a job is to be done, particularly in restoration work. A few kind words, genuine interest in the problem, and intelligent questions can often bring them around to your way of thinking.

If, however, a workman continues to make the same mistakes in spite of explanations and praise, insist that the contractor replace him with someone qualified to do the work. If you have a good contractor, he will be as concerned as you are with poor workmanship. When work must be done over, it costs the contractor money and eats into his profit. However, you should not expect perfection in a renovation; you are dealing with an old house that may have had flaws in it from the day it was built. A contractor cannot be expected to make an old floor absolutely level unless you are willing to pay him to rip it out and start all over again, from beams through subflooring.

When the finish begins, start making checklists of work done improperly and items missed. Give the list to the contractor at the beginning of each week. Continue until everything has been corrected. Keep a notebook and pencil in your pocket: only if you write things down will you remember all of them when talking to the contractor. You might even make a list of things you want to check while at the job.

Do not issue final payment until the job meets with your ap-

proval: trying to get a contractor back to rehang a door or change a faulty lock after he has been paid can be more difficult then making a child take bad-tasting medicine.

Occasionally an honest and dependable contractor will find himself in the awkward position of having underbid the job. This is a difficult situation for both contractor and owner, one that requires finesse and common sense.

If you are basically happy with the work that is being done and would like to see the contractor continue, you may have to be flexible about the cost of the job. Contractor and owner should discuss the problem to see if an equitable solution can be worked out. Point out that you had expected to pay only the given price for the work, which was the reason the contractor was hired. However, realize that in renovation there are sometimes unforeseen difficulties; you must either be willing to spend a little more or eliminate some items in order to get the job done. Changing contractors would probably mean going over the budget to finish the job, so if you are satisfied with the contractor, you might be better off continuing with him and paying him some additional money. If you remain rigid, demanding that the terms of the contract be fulfilled to the letter, the contractor may cut corners detrimental to your interest or walk off the job.

However, if you are unhappy with the contractor and his work is not acceptable and he is not following the construction documents and the contract, the only sensible solution is to get rid of him, and the earlier in the job you do it, the easier it will be.

• Terminating a Construction Contract

It would seem a simple matter to get rid of a contractor who has not lived up to the terms of the contract, but it is easier said than done.

The termination of a construction contract can be likened to a divorce: the longer it is postponed, the more deeply involved the two parties become. The amount of debt to be settled at the time of contract termination is often difficult to determine, and the owner can be liable for the full amount of the contract under certain circumstances. If the owner has paid the contractor the full amount due at a given point but the contractor has failed to pay workmen and suppliers, these men can demand payment from the owner up to the full amount of the contract price. In such a case, the owner becomes involved in litigation that is costly and time-consuming.

It is generally easier to determine the value of the work completed in the early phases of construction than toward the end. The payment schedule provided in the contract is one basis for settlement when terminating the contract. By signing the contract, you have given the contractor the right to receive the amount of money specified at any given stage. (This is one reason for making sure the payment schedule does not provide too much money in advance of work completed.)

As an example, take the following payment schedule for a $20,000 renovation job:

$2,000 on signing of contract
$4,000 on completion of demolition
$6,000 on completion of rough plumbing and wiring
$6,000 on completion of plastering
$2,000 on completion of all work

Should the contract be terminated before any work has begun, the owner would forfeit the $2,000 he had paid on the signing of the contract. (A lawsuit could possibly recoup some of this money, but legal fees and court costs would probably be as much as could be obtained from a settlement.) If the contract were terminated at the end of demolition, the contractor would be entitled to an additional $4,000 by the terms of the contract. As work progresses further, it becomes more difficult to determine how much work has been done. Determining the amount owed to the contractor can thus become a hassle.

Besides making a financial settlement, the owner must get a signed *release* from the contractor to legally terminate the agreement. Unless there is a release, the contractor can tie up the property in legal actions and prevent work from being completed. In the release the contractor relinquishes any rights he has under the terms of the contract. Since he would still be liable under the terms of the contract, the contractor generally will not sign a release unless he receives a release from the owner giving up any claims he might have against the contractor under the terms of the contract. This means that the owner takes full responsibility for work already done; if work is defective, the owner must assume the burden of repair or replacement.

A release will enable the owner to get someone else to finish the job, but finding another contractor may be difficult. The new contractor will be responsible for another's work, which may not be satisfactory. The second contractor will often charge a premium price for finishing someone else's job. The less work that has been done, the easier it is for the new man. If work has progressed too far, the owner may have to hire individual workmen to finish the job. In this case, there is usually no guarantee of the work, and the owner must take the consequences if there are problems.

As you can see, getting rid of a contractor once you have hired him is far from simple. Hire only a reputable contractor so you can avoid the problem. However, should you hire a contractor who proves unsatisfactory, terminate the contract as soon as possible, discussing procedure with your lawyer in advance of any action. Always be sure that the contract you sign has provision for termination and that you are provided with maximum protection if the clause is invoked.

• Liens

Even when the owner has a signed release from the contractor terminating the contract, workmen and suppliers whose materials and labor went into the work can come to the owner for payment of unpaid bills, although the contractor has been paid for the work. At any point during construction a man who has not been paid can place a lien on the property for the amount owed to him if he has been unable to collect. This puts the owner in the awkward position of being liable for bills he has already paid.

Placing a lien is usually a simple matter. For an owner to remove a lien he feels is unjustified is often not so simple. Lien laws vary from state to state but all liens must be filed within a fixed time after the work is completed and are valid only for a specified period. In New York, for example, a mechanic's lien stands for one year. At the end of that year the lien must be renewed. At the end of the second year the lien is automatically dropped if court proceedings have not been instituted to collect the debt. If an owner feels the lien is unjustified, he can sit out the two-year period and wait for the lienor to go to court. However, the owner may not be in a position to wait. If he has a construction loan, the bank probably will not issue further payments until the lien is removed. If the owner plans to refinance or sell the property, the lien usually has to be removed before either transaction takes place. To remove a lien, the owner must institute court proceedings, a costly and time-consuming affair, or pay it off.

Martha Stamm had a lien for $750 placed on one of her properties, which probably would have been thrown out in a court of law. However, the renovation was being financed by a construction loan and the bank refused to issue another payment until the lien was removed. Her lawyer agreed the lien was unwarranted but told her she had no choice but to pay it if she wanted the house finished on schedule. The alternative was to shut down the job, institute court proceedings, wait the year or more it would take the case to come to trial, and pay a minimum of five hundred dollars in legal fees and court costs to have the lien dismissed. Her lawyer suggested negotiations for settlement, and she ended by paying the lienor five hundred dollars to remove the lien. Her lawyer called it legal blackmail. Several years later, when another unwarranted lien was placed on one of Martha's properties, the bank agreed to let her put up the amount of the lien in an escrow fund in lieu of paying it off or going to court to have it removed. At the end of a year, when the lien was dropped, the bank returned the escrowed funds.

Most liens are the result of the contractor's failure to pay bills he owes, with the poor owner caught in a trap if he has already paid the contractor. If the owner keeps close tabs on the job from the very beginning, he will soon find out if bills are not being paid because the workmen will often tell him. Every owner should check with major suppliers and subcontractors before issuing a payment to the contractor. A clause can even be inserted in the construction contract requiring the contractor to provide *waivers of lien* from every subcontractor and supplier before a payment is issued. The waiver of lien relinquishes the right of the signer to lien the property for work done to that date.

If a workman, subcontractor, or supplier has not been paid, the owner cannot simply pay the man and deduct the money from the amount he pays the contractor. The owner has a contract with the contractor and must make all payments through him. If he makes payments to the contractor's employees, he is still liable to the contractor for the amount owed him.

James Greene had an unfortunate and infuriating experience with a contractor in his house in Manhattan's Chelsea. The workman failed to complete work contracted for, and Greene withheld payment. This contractor was in trouble with the Internal Revenue Service for nonpayment of back taxes. When the IRS pressed him for payment, the contractor informed the IRS that, according to the contract, he was owed several thousand dollars by Greene. Three months later, the IRS came to Greene demanding that he pay to them the amount owed the contractor. When he objected on the grounds that the money was not owed because the contract was not fulfilled, the IRS agent said that since Greene had not filed suit against the contractor within ninety days, he had no legal claim against the contractor and must pay the contractor's debt or face penalties himself.

This is an unusual story, but it did happen. It shows how important it is to know your rights and responsibilities.

• TIPS FOR RENOVATORS

Anyone who has ever done a renovation has advice to give beginners. Each has had problems he would like to warn others about or solutions he would like to pass along. The tips that follow are insignificant when compared to the preceding general information. However, where applicable, they may save you time, energy, and possibly money. And anything that makes renovation easier is always worthwhile.

• PROTECTING ITEMS IN THE HOUSE

Damage to things in the house (items to be salvaged and items already installed) is common during construction. Workmen can be totally insensitive in this area. They consider the house a construction site, where cigarettes are put out on the floor and walls are used to make notes about the job. They often forget to change their habits once the finish has begun. Following are some precautions you should take:

1. Before work begins, remove all mirrors, hardware,

and whatever else you plan to reuse; they may disappear or get broken during construction.

2. If you plan to salvage some items and get rid of others, clearly label each item that is to remain, either with paint or felt-tipped pen: "SAVE," "REUSE IN MASTER BEDROOM," and so forth.

3. When tearing out moldings and other items which match those that will remain in parts of the house, save a few to use in patching what is to stay. This applies to flooring and all woodwork.

4. If you plan to use existing wood floors, see that they are covered with building paper from the very beginning of construction. Plumbers have a way of setting up their pipe-cutting and -threading machines in the middle of parquet floors, spilling oil on them. Plasterers drop wet plaster on floors, burning the wood. Even if the floor is to be refinished, a thin parquet can take only a limited amount of sanding, and on other floors stains may be too deep for sanding to remove.

5. Cover all new floors as soon as they are laid. Use building paper, and see that it is taped down.

6. Quarry tile and other unglazed ceramic tile absorb liquids and dirt. Be sure that a sealer is applied immediately after installation, or stains may occur before renovation is complete.

7. Be sure all tubs are completely covered as soon as they are installed, because workmen will be climbing in and on them to plaster, paint, and install plumbing trim. Plumbers should do the covering by applying paper with a flour-and-water paste.

8. Protect your own tools, preferably under lock and key. Any tools left lying around may be used by a workman who may not be as careful with them as you would be, and often they will end up in his tool box.

9. Do not bring items such as hardware and electrical fixtures into the house until they can be installed; they

could get damaged or misplaced. Burglaries in unoc-
cupied houses under construction are also common.

10. When in doubt about damage to any item, cover it—
and cover everything you do not want painted before
the painter arrives on the job.

• PLASTERING

Most renovators are involved with plastering even if new
walls are made of sheetrock. When old walls or ceilings are
to remain, there is usually patching or repair to be done.
Since lime, the base for plaster, must be soaked overnight,
plaster cannot be mixed on a whim the way spackle can.
For this reason, all plastering should be done at the same
time. Here are some suggestions about plastering:

1. If part of a ceiling or wall is in bad condition, the workman can often knock out the bad plaster and replace it
without having to replace the whole wall or ceiling.

2. New plaster will not adhere properly to old plaster, especially if it has been painted. However, there are bonding agents that can be applied to old surfaces before
applying new plaster. These are usually available at
large paint and hardware stores.

3. Decorative moldings and ceiling medallions are often
missing or damaged. Plaster moldings can sometimes be
duplicated by putting together various pieces of
wooden moldings; when they are painted, no one but
you will know the difference. Reproductions of old
moldings, medallions and other decorative elements are
available from a number of sources.

4. Where small pieces of simple plaster moldings are missing or damaged, a simple mold can be made to dupli-
cate them. The procedure is as follows:

   a. The damaged molding is removed, and the plaster
   underneath is coated with a bonding agent.

   b. A small section of good molding is coated with vegetable shortening. A handful of wet plaster of Paris is then run across the greased surface to make a mold.

   c. After the mold has completely dried, the inside is coated with shortening.

   d. Globs of wet plaster are applied to the area where the molding is missing. The mold is then run along this plaster to form the missing molding.

   e. Any excess plaster is removed and the whole area smoothed with a wet brush.

   It often takes several tries to make this method work. The end result may not be perfect, but when the whole room is painted, the new molding will blend into the old.

5. Be sure that the plasterer does not leave holes around electrical boxes that will not be covered by fixtures and switch plates. The same is true around windows, doors, and floors.

6. Be sure that all plastering is done before the plasterer leaves the job.

• FINISHING DETAILS

The finishing details in your house can make the difference between a good job and a sloppy one, both in terms of the items selected and the way they are installed. A cheap doorknob on a carefully refinished mahogany door stands out like a dirty face on a child in a velvet party dress. Pay attention to finishing details when planning the renovation, and then check the job constantly during the finish to make sure that work is being done properly. The following are a few suggestions:

1. Be sure that moldings around windows and doors in the same room are alike. If you are creating a new opening and cannot match the existing trim, rip it all off and replace it with new moldings.

2. If you would like to have built-in storage in your

closets, plan for it when determining closet sizes. Inexpensive drawer units designed to be built into closets are available from Sears Roebuck and other places. These come in standard sizes, so you must plan the closets accordingly.

3. Do not forget about rods and shelves for closets. Galvanized plumbing pipes make excellent rods. They are heavier than those purchased at hardware stores.

4. Additional room for storage can sometimes be found in odd places. When bathrooms are wider than five feet, the space at the end of the tub is usually boxed in so the tub can be recessed. If this space is wider than twelve inches, it can be used for storage. If the space is too deep for your needs, it can be shortened.

5. Workmen have a way of making new ceilings eight feet, even if specified differently, because that is the standard ceiling height in new construction. Specify ceiling height, and then be sure the specs are followed.

6. Stock doors come in a wide variety of sizes and designs: Flush doors have either hollow or solid cores, with the former being the least expensive: paneled doors are more expensive than flush doors. (Hollow-core doors should never be used for exteriors.) Standard door heights are 6' 8" and 7' with thicknesses of 1⅜" or 1¾". Exterior doors should always be 1¾" doors.

7. Stock moldings can be applied to flush doors to give them a custom look. This applies to cabinet doors as well.

8. Many building codes require that entrance doors be equipped with one-way viewers (peepholes). This is a good idea even if not required, because it enables you to see who is at the door before opening it.

9. New straight oak flooring should be laid in the opposite direction from the flooring underneath for added strength. Flooring is normally laid lengthwise in the house, because beams run across the house. If your

flooring is being put on top of existing floors, the floor man will probably lay it lengthwise from habit and because it requires less cutting. Flooring laid widthwise in a hall will make the hall seem wider. Specify the direction in which new flooring is to be laid—then be present when it is installed to see that specs are followed. Floor layers often ignore specs, particularly when it saves them work.

10. Improper floor finishing causes owners a great deal of grief. The floor must be properly sanded before the finish is applied, and all finishes except wax require steel wooling between coats to remove bubbles and other imperfections. Floors should have at least two coats of finish, and three coats are preferable. The newer plastic finishes such as Fabulon and polyurethane (used on bowling alleys) are extremely durable and can be cleaned with a damp mop. To be sure you are satisfied with your wood floors, select a floor finisher who knows his business and can advise you on the different kinds of stains and finishes available.

11. In bad weather your floors and carpets can get messed up by wet boots and shoes. Small mats for wiping feet are often ignored by children and delivery men. Try recessing a large cocoa mat in the vestibule, where feet will be automatically wiped when people walk across it. This can save innumerable hours of cleaning.

12. If there are balusters (spindles) missing from your staircase, don't panic. If they are to be naturally finished, you must search for matching ones in the same wood. However, if you plan to paint them, new ones can be turned out by a local woodworking shop for very little money.

13. Mirrors and towel bars combined with appropriate wallpaper can give elegance to an ordinary bath. Be imaginative and you can work miracles on a very modest budget. Old mirrors in decorative frames can replace institutional medicine-chest mirrors, and wood-

en drapery rods with pineapple finials make fine towel bars when painted.

14. The location and kinds of bathroom accessories must be planned. Two soap dishes at different heights are nice for the family that uses a tub for both baths and showers. Toothbrush and glass holders are not particularly attractive and can often be tucked away out of sight by mounting them on the inside of a vanity door.

15. Plumbing trim is chrome-plated brass. It is possible to have the chrome removed for the same effect as expensive gold-plated faucets for a fraction of the price—particularly effective on simple institutional-looking trim. When selecting faucets, you might look at the lines used by hospitals; they can give a lavatory a sleek, contemporary look.

- WOOD STRIPPING

A favorite occupation with renovators everywhere, stripping woodwork can be quite an ordeal. The job is not done when the paint or varnish has been removed; the wood must also be sanded and finished. Be realistic about the amount of stripping you do, and be selective about what you strip. Some woodwork actually looks better painted. In the Victorian era, oak and mahogany were sometimes used as pine and fir are used today: You may find oak or mahogany that was painted from its very installation.

Once you have selected those items to be stripped, finish one item before starting the next, or you may find yourself sick of stripping without a single finished product. Do not put off stripping stationary objects until your house is finished. Paint remover takes off new as well as old paint, and floor finishes too.

For those who have not been discouraged, here are some pointers:

1. Shellac and some varnishes can be removed with alcohol. Try alcohol before using paint remover.

2. Use thick remover (called paste) for paint, and thin remover (called liquid) for varnish and the final application on painted surfaces.

3. Varnish will often roll off the wood when liquid remover is applied properly. Use a brush loaded with remover, and lay (rather than brush) it on—varnish smears when brushed. To remove loosened varnish, use a putty knife, and scrape from top to bottom or wash it away with another application of remover.

4. Apply paste liberally to painted surfaces, and let it stand long enough to eat away the paint. If there is much paint to remove, you will have to make many applications.

5. Doors or other items that can be taken down should be placed in a horizontal position for stripping. The remover can lie on flat surfaces long enough to work well; it tends to roll off vertical surfaces.

6. Invest in two sawhorses, and lay items to be stripped across them. Be sure sawhorses are the proper height so you can work in a comfortable position.

7. Get the proper tools: an old aluminum saucepan to hold paint remover, putty knives of various sizes (be sure to get one small enough to fit all surfaces of paneled doors and other details—your hardware store can cut down a larger one to any size you need), cheap paintbrushes, steel wool, rags or paper towels.

8. If you are doing much stripping, buy paint remover by the case, and try to get a discount on each case. You will be amazed at how much remover is required just to strip a door. You might want to buy paper towels by the case also, or start collecting rags from all your friends—you will never have enough yourself to supply the need.

9. Use rubber gloves—paint remover is disastrous to the hands. Wear safety glasses to protect your eyes, and work in a well-ventilated area.

10. Paint scrapers should be used first to remove any

loose, cracked, or peeling paint. They are available at hardware stores in various sizes; be sure to get the ones with replaceable blades, and get extra packages of blades. Take as much paint off as possible with the scraper before applying remover.

11. Apply paint remover to a small area at a time. Paint remover dries up and becomes gummy if it stands too long. When working on vertical surfaces, start from the top and work down to keep stripped surfaces from smearing.

12. For the tiny grooves and crevices use nut picks (they resemble dental tools and come packaged with many nutcrackers) or long nails to scrape out paint.

13. After remover has stood long enough to soften paint, scrape the surface with a putty knife to remove both paint and remover. Wipe surface clean before next application.

14. Steel wool can be used to remove stubborn paint. Apply remover, let stand, and scrub with steel wool.

15. When the surface is free of paint and varnish, wash the whole area with liquid remover and wipe it clean with a clean soft rag or paper towel.

16. Once wood is stripped, cover it completely until you are ready to sand and finish it. Raw wood will stain and get dirty, so be sure the covering is taped down.

17. Removable pieces, such as shutters, are sometimes stripped by dipping in a vat of lye. We urge that you NEVER strip wood in lye, or even buy pieces that have been stripped in lye, because the wood will be irrevocably damaged.

18. There is an electric paint-removing tool that is fast and effective. An open heating coil with a wooden handle, it becomes red-hot within a few minutes after being plugged in. When held near the painted surface, it quickly causes paint to loosen so that it almost falls away at the touch of a paint scraper, often in hand-sized flakes, even out of grooved areas. The dry resi-

due can be swept up, unlike the sticky wet mess from paint remover that can ruin your floors as well as your hands. This tool (called the HYDElectric Paint Remover) is nowhere near as hazardous as a torch, or as likely to scorch your woodwork, but it should be used with reasonable care. (Only sanding will remove scorch. If scorching is deep, it may be impossible to sand sufficiently without distorting the piece. You can paint the scorched wood, but there is a chance that the scorch will bleed through.)

Another electric paint stripper called a heat gun, which resembles a hair dryer, is particularly effective for detailed carving.

19. Finishes for wood include shellac, varnish, linseed oil, and wax. If stain is to be used, it is applied first; but the wood should have a protective coating other than the stain. A stained varnish does both jobs at once.

20. Raw wood normally requires more than one application of finish. In the case of linseed oil, varnish, and shellac, the surface should be rubbed with fine steel wool before the second coat is applied, since these finishes often raise the grain of the wood. Wax or linseed oil finishes need additional applications periodically to keep the wood protected.

· PAINTING

There is more to painting than just wielding a paintbrush. Unless walls are new plaster, much preparation must be done before the paint is applied. If you hire a painter to do the work, watch him closely if you are at all particular about the way your house looks. Following are some suggestions about painting, whether you hire someone to do it or do it yourself:

1. Spackling compound for patching holes and cracks comes in powdered form or ready-mixed. The latter is more expensive but far easier to use.

288 · *Buying and Renovating a House in the City*

2. Be sure all telephone wires, nails, and so forth are removed before painting is begun. Painters often paint right over them even if told to remove them.
3. Remove all hardware before the painter goes to work. No matter how careful he is, paint will surely get on doorknobs and other fixtures. Do not let the painter paint over door latches, because they will not work properly afterward. Either remove them or cover them with masking tape.
4. If light-switch and outlet plates are not to be painted, remove them. If walls are to be white, you can get white covers with baked-on finish, but you must specifiy them.
5. If possible, have all lighting fixtures installed after the painting is complete to avoid any chance of getting paint on them.
6. Take all naturally finished doors off the hinges and store them in another room while painting is being done. This is usually much easier than covering them.
7. All woodwork that is to remain unpainted should be covered and taped to be sure that no paint gets on the wood—this includes kitchen cabinets.
8. Be sure that all floors are covered and edges taped, even floors that will be finished after painting is complete. Removing paint from raw wood requires extra sanding and is particularly difficult around the edges.
9. Specify in your contract that the painter remove any paint from windows and mirrors, and unstick all windows.
10. Use ready-mix paint wherever possible. If paint must be custom mixed, the color can be chosen from a book of color chips that are carefully catalogued and can be duplicated at any future date so long as you keep the catalogue number. If you or your painter mix the color, you will probably be unable to match it later.
11. Use semigloss (satin) paint on wood trim and doors because you can wash it more easily than flat paint.

You might even want to use semigloss on walls for the same reason—the finish dulls very quickly.

12. Using light colored paint in rooms that are dark makes them brighter. It's amazing what white paint can do for a room that gets little natural light.

13. If you are doing any painting yourself with oil-base paints, we would like to pass on to you a marvelous time-saving tip. When you must stop working before your job is complete, simply wrap your brush or roller in aluminum foil and put it in your freezer until you need it again. It will not affect the other contents of the freezer, and when you take it out and unwrap it, you will find it in exactly the same condition as when you put it there, except for being a trifle chilly! This enables you to do a bit of work whenever you have a spare moment without worrying about the nuisance of brush cleaning.

14. To keep paint from running down sides of the can while you are painting, make nail holes through the lip of the can in several places so that the paint will drip back into the can.

15. To prevent paint dripping down brush handles onto your hands and arms, cut the end off a baby bottle nipple and insert the brush handle. Unfortunately, nipples will only fit on smaller brushes.

• LIVING IN A HOUSE UNDER CONSTRUCTION

Living amidst a renovation is not everyone's cup of tea. Most who do so act out of necessity. Being greeted by workmen when you awake and living with constant plaster dust are part of the ordeal, but life can be easier if a little advance planning is done. The following tips are for people contemplating residence in a construction site:

1. Have all good furniture put in storage. The cost may seem unnecessary, but otherwise your furniture may be worth nothing by the time renovation is complete.

2. Pack everything but the barest essentials in boxes and store out of the workmen's way until work has been finished. Too many "things" get in the way and have to be shifted constantly.
3. Set up housekeeping in an area where the least amount of work is to be done. That way you can achieve some feeling of permanence while renovation progresses and will not have to move constantly from one room to another as work is being done.
4. You may want to move out of the house for a week or so while plumbing is being installed. The plumber will not have to work around your plumbing needs, and the job can be done more quickly. The cost of a hotel room for a week is usually a small price to pay to avoid the inconvenience of no hot water, or no water at all.
5. Remember that it is just as difficult for workmen to work with people in the house as it is for you to live with the construction. When you are considerate of their problems, they will usually be considerate of yours. Let all contractors who are bidding on the job know that you plan to live in the house. Discuss with them how to schedule the work so there is a minimum of inconvenience to everyone.

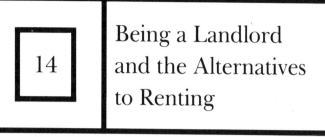

14 Being a Landlord and the Alternatives to Renting

BEING THE LANDLORD of a house you live in is scarcely more difficult than maintaining the whole house for yourself. The owner has the same responsibilities whether he occupies the entire house or has tenants: the property must be maintained in compliance with the local building code, the sidewalk must be swept and snow shoveled, the lawn mowed, and garbage taken care of in accordance with local regulations. The landlord is, of course, responsible for maintaining the rental units and any public areas, but if he occupied this space himself, he would have the same responsibility.

The main burden of being a landlord is in renting the apartments, keeping good relations with tenants, and collecting the rent each month. When you consider that these tenants are helping you pay for your house, the work scarcely seems like much. If you do not wish to take on this job, a professional management firm can be hired to operate the house for you, allowing you to live there as a tenant yourself.

Most renovators choose to do their own renting and managing, and have seldom had difficulty with either. They normally design apartments in which they would be willing to live themselves and are often far more imaginative in planning rental units than the average real estate investor, who looks solely at the economics of the situation. There are myriad ways in which renovators have found their tenants (there are real estate brokers who will be glad to rent your apartments for you; and if apartments happen to be scarce, the tenant pays the broker's fee and it costs you nothing for this service), but the most common procedure is advertising in the newspaper.

· HOW TO RENT AN APARTMENT

Make the advertisement appealing to the type of tenant you are seeking, and list the price of the apartment (or you may spend the day turning away people who had not planned to spend as much as you are asking). A typical advertisement might read as follows:

1-bedroom apartment in renovated town house. Fireplace, modern bath, and kitchen. House lovingly restored by owner-occupant. $350/mo.

Such an advertisement describes the apartment and tells the prospective tenant that he will have the security of living in an owner-occupied house, often a plus in areas where renovation has just begun. It also lets the reader know that the owner cares about the apartment.

The advertisement should also state the area in which the apartment is located. You might even want to give the exact address and have an open house for prospective tenants. In any case, be sure to list a phone number where people can call to get information and make an appointment to see the apartment.

The condition the apartment is in can be all-important in renting. Even if the apartment is not complete when you begin showing it, be sure it is clean and neat. A dirty bathroom or unwashed windows can detract from its charm. You will expect your tenant to take care of your apartment—show him you care by having it in good condition when he first sees it.

The most important factor in renting an apartment is checking on prospective tenants. Remember, you are selecting a tenant, not making a lifelong friend. Your first concern is that he is able to pay the rent and has a record of prompt payment. Other concerns are his stability and reliability: you do not want a tenant who moves in today and out tomorrow. You also want him to take care of your apartment and not be a constant source of noise and annoyance. If an applicant meets these qualifications, you should have a good tenant.

Any interested person should fill out an application for the apartment and leave a deposit of one month's rent, refundable if the applicant is not accepted. Julius Blumberg, Inc., makes standard application forms (available from 80 Exchange Place, New York, N.Y., 10004 or at large stationery stores), or you can make your own application form. Here is the information you need:

1. Name and address of applicant
2. Name and address of current landlord
3. Name and address of employer and how long employed there
4. Name and address of bank(s).
5. Charge accounts or other credits references (at least two)

Check all references carefully. Investigating tenants in advance of accepting them will prevent problems in the future. You certainly do not want a tenant who has a record of bouncing checks or unpaid bills. If an applicant does not seem reliable, refund his deposit and look elsewhere.

In order to keep the relationship between you and your tenant on a business basis, you should require both a lease and a security deposit before he moves in.

- SECURITY

Security (usually in the amount of one month's rent) is a deposit given to the landlord to cover damage to the apartment or loss of income if the tenant breaks his lease. The security is held until the tenant moves out and the landlord has an opportunity to inspect the apartment. It does not cover normal wear and tear on the apartment, but is for repairs that have to be made as the result of the tenant's carelessness or neglect. Under no circumstances should the security deposit be accepted as the final month's rent; it is refunded to the tenant after he has vacated.

- LEASES

Leases are for the protection of both landlord and tenant. They set down the rights and responsibilities of each party. Leases can be written for any length of time mutually agreeable, but one to two years is the term of a typical apartment lease. Standard-form leases are available at most large stationery stores or directly from Julius Blumberg, Inc.

Be sure that the lease you use does *not* contain a *sublet clause*. The sublet clause allows the tenant to move out of the apartment if he can find another tenant willing to sublet the apartment for the remainder of the lease. You may want to include a clause that provides for landlord approval of a sublet tenant, but the straight sublet clause allows your tenant to select the new tenant for you, causing you to lose some control over your house. If a prospective tenant is subject to transfer or feels that he may be unable to fulfill the term of the lease, you can give him the right to break the lease with thirty to ninety days' written notice and the forfeit of his security if no new tenant is found during this period. This method is far preferable to a sublet clause, but any such agreement must be incorporated in the lease.

The names and number of occupants of the apartment should be included in the lease. If the apartment is rented to two unmarried people, it is best to have the lease in both names so that both are responsible. And of course, you do not want to find out that the apartment you thought you were renting to one person is to be occupied by several. When selecting a tenant, keep in mind the size of the apartment. Too many people in too small a space are bound to create problems such as excessive noise and abnormal wear and tear.

There should be two copies of the signed lease, one for you and one for your tenant. At the time the lease is signed, you should receive the security deposit and one month's rent in advance. At the same time, the tenant should be made aware of his responsibilities. The policy of garbage removal should be explained, along with any other rules and regulations. If the tenant is to pay his own utility bills, he should be told to contact the utility companies to make provisions for the meters to be put in his name.

You should make clear from the very beginning what you expect of your tenant; do not hesitate to see that he lives up to the terms of his lease. On the other hand, be sure that you live up to your responsibilities as a landlord. You cannot expect to have a good tenant if you are not a good landlord.

• HOW TO BE A GOOD LANDLORD

There are no rules for being a good landlord, but if you treat your tenants as you would want to be treated, you should have no problems. Keep your house in good condition, and make repairs promptly. If a problem arises that you cannot solve immediately, keep your tenant informed. Most tenants are sympathetic and will be patient if they know you are trying to get the repair made.

The following is a list of things that good landlords do:

1. Keep public areas clean (halls and the front and rear of the house).
2. Promptly shovel snow from sidewalks and exterior stairs.
3. Have an adequate number of garbage cans (if you provide them), and see that the area where garbage is stored is kept clean.
4. Replace light bulbs in public areas as soon as they burn out.
5. Provide plenty of heat and hot water.
6. Always be pleasant to your tenants.

• THE ALTERNATIVES TO RENTING

There is another way to handle space that you do not plan to occupy yourself—rather than rent, you can sell it. This can be done in one of several ways:

1. By selling an interest in the property to one or more people who will live in the other apartment(s).
2. By converting the house into a cooperative.
3. By converting the house into a condominium.

These alternatives should be discussed thoroughly with a knowledgeable attorney who can explain them, advise you, and perform the legal duties of the transaction.

A complete discussion of these different forms of ownership is far beyond the scope of this book, but there are a few things you should know when considering selling rather than renting.

If you are the sole owner of the house, you have sole authority to make all decisions yourself; if not, when you sell, you must share the decision-making, that is, your partner(s) or co-owner(s) may not want to spend money to paint the exterior or you may differ on what color it should be painted. On the other hand, you have others with whom to share the responsibilities and liabilities.

When you sell rather than rent, you recoup some or all of your cash investment. In return, you must pay your fair share of the operating costs of the house. When you have rental apartments in the house, you should pay a smaller amount of rent for your apartment than your tenants do because you have a cash investment in the house and are responsible for operating and maintaining it. In selling, you lose this advantage, along with certain tax benefits available to owners of rental property. (See Appendix, page 301 for tax benefits.)

The decision to sell or rent is a purely personal one—there are advantages and disadvantages in each situation. Your financial status may determine the choice. If the amount of cash you have is small, selling may be the answer. And when the purchase and renovation of a house is beyond your means, it is possible to buy a house with one or more people and make it a joint venture from the beginning.

Veleno

Made in the USA
Columbia, SC
10 March 2022

57477429R00186

Appendix

- INCOME TAX BENEFITS

Real estate owners are allowed income tax deductions for the following:

1. Money paid for real estate taxes and interest on mortgages
2. Expenses incurred in operating income property
3. Depreciation of income property

- REAL ESTATE TAXES AND INTEREST ON MORTGAGES

Whether the house is urban or suburban, a private home or an income-producing property, real estate taxes and the interest paid on mortgages can be deducted from your personal income for federal, state, and city income taxes *provided* the house is in your name. (If the property is in a corporate name, it is the corporation that derives these and all other tax benefits.) Your tax bracket will determine how beneficial these deductions are, but even those in a low tax bracket will derive some tax savings. For example, if you are in a 20% bracket, you will save 20% on all money spent for tax-deductible items—that is, you will not have to pay any tax on that money.

For some people, the income tax bite can be the major motivation for buying and renovating a house. People who earn above-average salaries find the lion's share going to pay income tax. Investing in a house therefore represents a double saving to them: their monthly rent goes partly into their investment (amortization on mortgages) and partly into tax-deductible interest and real estate taxes.

• OPERATING EXPENSES OF RENTAL PROPERTY

Income from property will raise the owner's personal income, but he can deduct from his rental income the expenses incurred in producing it. When figuring operating costs for tax purposes, mortgage amortization payments are not included. The following is a list of operating expenses that are deductible:

1. Heat
2. Utilities for public areas and for tenants' apartments *if* the owner pays utility charges
3. Water and sewer charges
4. Insurance
5. Maintenance and repairs (labors and materials)
6. Management costs, if paid to someone else

If the entire house is rented, all these expenses are deductible. However, if the owner lives in part of the house, he may not deduct the listed expenses for operating his apartment. In such a case, he may deduct a portion of these expenses commensurate with the amount of rented space—that is, if half of the house is rented, 50% of the expenses are deductible.

• DEPRECIATION

An additional bonus to owners of income property comes in the form of depreciation. The technical definition of depreciation is the loss of value in real property brought about by age, physical deterioration, or functional or economic obsolescence. This means that the value of the building may be taken as an expense over an extended period of time (what the Internal Revenue Service calls the reasonable life of the building). Depreciation is figured in a dollar amount deductible yearly from the value of the property for tax purposes; it is a noncash expense, or what is commonly referred to as a tax shelter. Here is how depreciation works:

An owner figures the cost of the property, exclusive of land. (Land is not depreciable because it does not lose value through age, deterioration, and so on.) Then he must estimate the percentage of the building that is rented if he occupies part of the house himself; the rented percentage becomes the *base for depreciation.* If 100% of the house is rented, 100% of the value can be depreciated; if half of the house is rented, 50% of the value can be depreciated. *An owner cannot depreciate that portion of the house in which he lives.*

Once the base for depreciation has been figured, the period of depreciation must be established; for an older renovated house it is usually twenty to thirty years. The base of depreciation is then reduced over the period of depreciation, with the amount of the reduction taken as a tax-deductible expense of the property each year.

Depreciation over a twenty-year period is taken at 5% of the depreciable base, and for thirty years is taken at $3\frac{1}{3}\%$ per year; it is called *straight-line depreciation:* taking the same amount of depreciation each year. Another kind of depreciation is *accelerated depreciation,* in which a higher amount is deducted in the first years, with the amount diminishing yearly over the depreciation period. Whether to use straight-line or accelerated depreciation should be discussed with your lawyer or accountant, but for the purpose of this book, we will deal with straight-line depreciation. The following is an example:

A property cost the owner $50,000 to purchase and

renovate. The owner lives in half the house and rents the other half. The value of the land is $10,000, leaving $40,000 as the value of the house. Because half of the house is rented, $20,000 (50% of $40,000) is base for depreciation. The house will be depreciated over twenty years, enabling the owner to deduct as an expense $1,000 (5% of $20,000) each year for twenty years.

The theory behind depreciation is that at the end of the depreciation period the value of the property will be substantially reduced and will require an extensive investment in improvements in order to return it to its original value. Whether you agree or disagree with the theory, be sure to take advantage of the fact. Depreciation deductions can save you a great deal of money.

However, you should be aware that depreciation will have a tax effect when you sell the property. How much the property cost you is established when you first take depreciation, and is reduced by the amount of depreciation you deduct. On the property mentioned above, the owner's cost of $50,000 is reduced by $1,000 each year. Thus, if he were to sell it five years after he bought it, his cost for tax purposes would be $45,000 ($50,000 less the $5,000 already taken as a reduction in value). Therefore, if he sold for $50,000, he would make a profit of $5,000 on the sale as far as the Internal Revenue Service is concerned. He must now pay tax on the $5,000 which he has paid no tax on before. However, he will have less tax to pay at the time of sale, because the money is now capital gains rather than regular income.

- SPECIAL TAX CONSIDERATION FOR HISTORIC INCOME-PRODUCING PROPERTIES

In 1976 the U.S. Congress recognized the value of preserving historic properties. The Tax Reform Act of 1976 included special tax incentives to encourage people to renovate historic buildings as income-producing properties instead of tearing them down. The 1976 Tax Act has been replaced by the Economic Recovery Tax Act of 1981, which still contains special tax incentives for preserving historic income-producing properties (residential, commercial, or industrial). Although the tax incentives do not cover owner-occupied historic buildings, they can be used by owner-occupants to cover that portion which produces income. Complete coverage of these complex tax incentives is beyond the scope of this book. To get detailed information on the Economic Recovery Tax Act of 1981 and how to determine if a building qualifies as historic, contact your State Historic Preservation Office.

• REAL ESTATE TAXES

The assessed valuation *(tax assessment)* on property is the value set by the city* as a base for determining real estate taxes. The city has a *tax rate* that is applied to the assessment to determine the amount of real estate taxes levied against each property. The tax rate is often expressed in dollars per hundred dollars of assessed value. If the tax rate were five dollars per hunred dollars of value, the tax rate would be 5% of assessed value.

The amount of real estate taxes an owner must pay is based on the property's tax assessment and the current tax rate. A rise in taxes could be the result of either an increase in assessment, an increase in tax rate, or both. It is important for an owner to know his assessment so that he knows whether a property tax increase is based on a change in rate or a change in assessment. An owner can do nothing about an increase in rate, but it is often possible to do something about the assessment.

There is no universal policy on tax assessments, and you

---

*Technically not the city but the assessing unit, which might be a village, town, city, county—any or all of them together or separately.

may find that the policy varies in different areas of the same city. The tax assessor acts as an independent agent, and one assessor may be more diligent and conscientious than another. Whether your property will be reassessed as a result of renovation will in part be determined by past practice, though this is always subject to change. Some cities, such as Chicago, tend to give the renovator a break and make it a practice to let the assessment stand for several years after renovation is complete. Other places, like Manhattan, go to the other extreme and raise assessments at the first opportunity. Wherever you live, there is a better than even chance that there will be a reassessment as a result of renovation. A little research on your part should give you an idea of what to expect.

Tax assessments, a matter of public record, are on file at the tax assessor's office. A trip there might well be worth the time. If there is renovated property in the area, the prior assessments on this property will give an indication of whether it has been reassessed, when it was reassessed, and how much of an increase resulted. If renovated and unrenovated property have about the same assessment, then no reassessment has been made. When looking at the assessment records, make a note of the properties with exceptionally high assessments, and go by and look at them to see if you can determine the reason for the high assessment.

There are several general guidelines you ought to be aware of. Single-family homes normally have lower assessments than the same property containing rental units. Tax assessments often reflect the amount of income a property produces for the owner. A property that has been sold several times for an increased price will often have a higher assessment than one that has had the same owner for many years. If sale prices in an area have risen sharply, there is a good chance that all property in the area will be reassessed to reflect increased value. In some cities the assessment is broken down into land assessment and total assessment. If a reassessment is based on a renovation, the land assessment generally remains the same but the total assessment is raised to reflect the increased value of the house. If the whole area is reassessed because of a general rise in sale prices, it is often the land value that is increased. The assessment of land is based on the size of the lot, and the same standard is applied to all property on a given street or in a given area. In the case of building assessments, there is often a wide discrepancy in assessed value.

• You Can Protest Your Tax Assessment

Many property owners are not aware that they can protest their tax assessment. Each city has its own procedure for protest, but they follow a general pattern. Tax assessments are posted each year at a specified time. (You must find out when this happens in your city.) The tax assessor usually has a given period of time in which to make his reassessments. At the end of this time, an assessment for each piece of property is posted in the tax rolls. This is often done well in advance of the issuance of real estate tax bills; it is often too late to protest when the tax bill is received. (In some cities reassessment notices are mailed to affected property owners, but this is not true everywhere.) An owner must go to the tax assessor's office to find out if there has been a change in assessment. If an owner feels that an increase is unjustified, he can obtain a protest form from the tax assessor's office, which must be filed with the city by the date specified on the form. The owner is then given a hearing in which to state his case. If the city offers a reduction that is acceptable, this new assessment is entered in the tax books. If, however, no reduction is offered (or the reduction is insufficient), the owner can go to court with the case. However, a form must be filed to leave the protest open or reject the offer that has been made.

A protest of tax assessment should be discussed with your lawyer. The procedures are often complex, confusing, and difficult to follow. In many cities there are attorneys who specialize in tax protests. They normally work on a contingency basis—that is, you pay them nothing unless they save you money. These lawyers are thoroughly familiar with local tax policies and know what arguments to use at the time of the hearing. These attorneys are usually more effective than an owner can be. Your own lawyer should be able to provide the names of tax protest lawyers.

You usually cannot protest previous tax assessments, so be sure to file a protest the year of increase or the year you purchase if you feel the assessment is too high. You automatically accept the assessment if you do not protest, and it is hard to convince the assessor to reduce it the next year, even though you were not aware of your ability to object. Check the current assessment of the property when you buy it (along with the dates for posting new assessments and protesting assessments), and discuss with your lawyer whether it is too high in relation to the price you paid. As a neighborhood declines, so do property values, but the tax assessor seldom reduces assessment unless there is a protest. Tax assessments in a deteriorated neighborhood may be higher in relation to sale price than in other areas of the city. You generally have grounds to protest assessment based on the price you paid for your house, if the relationship of assessed value to market value differs from the general standard in the area.

- PROPERTY TAX ABATEMENT AND EXEMPTION

Some cities have a policy of tax abatement and/or exemption under certain conditions, such as for veterans, the elderly, or as an incentive for providing certain kinds of housing. These programs vary so from city to city that it is impractical to give specific information about them. You should check to see if abatement or exemption is available and under what conditions. Find out in advance, because these programs may affect the kind of house you buy and the renovation you do. Availability of tax abatement or exemption does not mean you will want to take advantage of them. Ask your lawyer if such programs are available in your area, and discuss with him their merits and disadvantages.

- INSURANCE

  The insurance that most homeowners need consists of coverage for fire and other damage to the house and its contents, injury to persons on the property (liability), and theft. All of this coverage is available to owners of one- and two-family houses in a package policy *(homeowner's policy)* at substantial savings. The same insurance for multiple dwellings (three families or more) is provided by several policies. *Rent insurance* to cover the loss of income and to provide quarters for the owner-occupant if the property must be vacated because of fire damage can be added to the homeowner's policy (and other fire policies) for a minimal charge.

  It is mandatory that you insure your house for the proper amount because of *co-insurance* requirements. To get a fair recovery in case of loss, you need an amount of insurance equal to 80% of the *reconstruction cost* of the house, less reasonable depreciation. In computing the value of your house, do not include the land. If your house has less than 80% coverage, you may, in case of partial loss, get "depreciation recovery" rather than the full amount needed to cover costs—for instance, as little as $5,000 or $6,000 after a $10,000 fire.

  The amount of insurance you carry should not be based only on what you actually spent on the house, but must also take into account increases in construction costs and property values. Consult an insurance broker in determining the proper amount of insurance to carry in order to avoid a co-insurance penalty.

Renovators sometimes have difficulty obtaining insurance on vacant houses and those under construction where there is added risk of fire and malicious mischief. A good insurance broker can solve many of these problems. However, in some renovation neighborhoods insurance is difficult to obtain regardless of the condition of the house. This is called redlining, a practice which is against public policy, and in many states it is illegal. If you suspect redlining, contact your State Insurance Department or Office of Consumer Affairs.

About the Authors

After a career in commercial art and illustration, DEIRDRE STANFORTH wrote several successful cookbooks on the Creole cuisine of her native New Orleans. Then she bought a brownstone in Manhattan. In the course of an extremely traumatic renovation, she met Martha Stamm, who was about to embark on her fifth renovation six blocks away.

Since first publication of *Buying and Renovating a House in the City,* Deirdre has written *Restored America,* with architectural photographer Louis Reens, which records "Cinderella stories" of restoration and recycling in every region of the country. She has participated in the creation of a pilot program for a television series based on *Restored America,* and has lectured on the subject coast-to-coast. A subsequent collaboration with Louis Reens produced another book about old buildings, *Romantic New Orleans.*

She has served as president of the Brownstone Revival Committee, and has returned to her original metier as a portrait painter. She and her husband still live in the brownstone that inspired the books and activities associated with them.

A college drop-out who chose marriage over finishing her last year of school, MARTHA STAMM CONNELL found both her vocation and her avocation when she bought her first brownstone. A renovator and renovation consultant, Martha bought and renovated 5 brownstones on West 78 St. in New York City before co-authoring this book. Continuing her renovation activities after she divorced and returned to her native Atlanta, Martha bought and renovated over a dozen houses in several of Atlanta's reviving neighborhoods. In addition to consulting, Martha served as president of the Atlanta chapter of the Victorian Society in America and as a member of the Board of Trustees of Atlanta Landmarks, Inc., the non-profit organization that rescued the "Fabulous" Fox Theatre from the wrecking ball and converted it from a deteriorating movie palace showing Grade B movies into a successful non-profit performing arts center. It was through her preservation activities that she met her second husband Arnall T. (Pat) Connell, Georgia Tech architecture professor and founder of Atlanta Landmarks, Inc. The Connells live in a house that Martha renovated.

Index

312 · *Index*